What people are sayi̠ ̠

The Hidden Goddess

This timely, robust and provocative examination of the pivotal and enduring place of Goddess within the Jewish and Christian faith traditions is deeply inspiring. Laurie Martin-Gardner's textual analysis brings a refreshing reframing of the continual presence, devotion to, and existence of Goddess despite the myriad attempts to destroy or hide her. This book brings to life the reality of Goddess, past and present. It is a valuable resource for scholars of all religions traditions and readers interested to know more about Goddess while simultaneously offering a powerful new perspective for Goddess loving readers.
Dr Lynne Sedgmore, CBE, Poetess, Priestess and Founder of Goddess Luminary Wheel

The Hidden Goddess is a readable and accessible antidote to the stereotype that the divine feminine is absent in the biblical traditions. A great resource for women and men seeking the Goddess in unlikely places.
Professor Mary Ann Beavis, Ph.D., Department of Religion and Culture, St. Thomas More College, Canada

This book is well researched and – which is a rare combination – also well written. I certainly recommend it for readers who like some solid history and research over flights of fancy.
Elisheva Nesher, AMHA USA Shophet

The Hidden Goddess

The Quest for the Divine Feminine in the Judeo-Christian Tradition - from Asherah to Mary Magdalene

The Hidden Goddess

The Quest for the Divine Feminine in the
Judeo-Christian Tradition - from Asherah to
Mary Magdalene

Laurie Martin-Gardner

**MOON
BOOKS**

Winchester, UK
Washington, USA

JOHN HUNT PUBLISHING

First published by Moon Books, 2020
Moon Books is an imprint of John Hunt Publishing Ltd., No. 3 East Street, Alresford
Hampshire SO24 9EE, UK
office@jhpbooks.net
www.johnhuntpublishing.com
www.moon-books.net

For distributor details and how to order please visit the 'Ordering' section on our website.

Text copyright: Laurie Martin-Gardner 2018

ISBN: 978 1 78535 908 8
978 1 78535 909 5 (ebook)
Library of Congress Control Number: 2018964466

A CIP catalogue record for this book is available from the British Library.

Design: Stuart Davies

UK: Printed and bound by CPI Group (UK) Ltd, Croydon, CR0 4YY
US: Printed and bound by Thomson-Shore, 7300 West Joy Road, Dexter, MI 48130

We operate a distinctive and ethical publishing philosophy in
all areas of our business, from our global network of authors to
production and worldwide distribution.

Contents

In loving memory of my mother.

Foreword

by Chantel Lysette

When Laurie told me that she was working on this project, my first response was that of pure elation. I knew she had been dreaming of this moment for a very long time and working even harder toward her goal. Of course, as a friend and colleague, I couldn't have been happier for her. In our many, lazy Sunday afternoon chats and dusk to dawn musings, we often found ourselves looking at the state of the world and asking, "What would the goddess do?" And as women punctuate international headlines with one great historical feat after another, I can't help but wonder if the millennium's surge of female empowerment is the Goddess's way of lighting the path and inspiring the world, albeit from her cloistered shadows.

The iron hand of mainstream religion is beginning to show stress fractures as women seek to find representation and equality on Earth *and* in Heaven. And as a Lutheran turned witch, turned Buddhist, turned Pentecostal, turned "no labels, please," I have been seeking out the goddess ever since I finally found the strength to embrace the notion that "our Father" was just that, the father. This, of course, sent me on a quest in search of "our Mother," and inevitably allowed me to cross paths with the kindred spirit that is Laurie Martin-Gardner, whose determination to discover the mother goddess seemed as much of an unrelenting spiritual quest, as it did an academic juggernaut.

Both Laurie and I write on spirituality and comparative religion. There is plenty of room in this field for anyone interested, but the rub is seeing, in writing and academic circles alike, how even the most casual or indirect indoctrination easily shades one's point-of-view, as well as hinders one's ability to even realize this deficient objectivity. And I truly believe that ofttimes, slant and bias isn't intentional, for I must admit, I've looked back at my previous works and seen how my years in the Christian church have swayed my work, despite my sincere and best efforts to break from its hold. Blessedly, Laurie doesn't have to fight against all the entanglements, snares and baggage of indoctrination—childhood years in Sunday school, or years of Solstice celebrations, for that matter. Having known Laurie for over a decade, I knew she could not be swayed by religious orthodoxy, nor shined by New Age charm. Her journey in finding the goddess would be wholly unadulterated.

Still, when one thinks of a goddess, various pop-culture images may come to mind, such as a fictional, sword-wielding warrior princess, a female television personality or an internet makeup guru with millions of followers worldwide. Thankfully, thoughts of mothers, sisters and wives aren't far behind. It seems that in the digital age when humanity has access to a record amount of information at record speed, "goddess" has come to mean many things to many people. But in the West, where the sex ratio of women to men is largely equal, the term hardly evokes images of divinity or instills a sense of transcendent awe, especially in mainstream religious circles. As we set full sail into the new millennium, the goddess has largely been relegated to entertainment, mythology and whims of fancy, a far fall from her historical seat that was once equal to her male counterpart.

In fact, when it comes to Judaism, Christianity, and Islam, she's nowhere to be found and scholars and clerics—male and female alike—often scoff at the notion of her existence. For the most part, religious acknowledgement of a goddess in the modern West falls upon the shoulders of the New Age movement, whose roots are intricately intertwined with ancient cults and practices that adopted the goddess long after she had been discarded by the founders of the very religions that now deny her presence in the temples, churches and mosques.

In *The Hidden Goddess*, Laurie Martin-Gardner—artist, writer, mother and ardent champion for the restoration of "plain, ol' fashioned common sense" (a.k.a. "using the brain God[dess] gave you")—goes on an adventured-filled quest in search of the ancient goddess, the divine feminine, the sacred feminine. Taking on the daunting task of poring through endless pages of ancient and religious texts, historical records and modern discourses, Martin-Gardner craftily pieces together an uncomplicated, yet thorough treatise on the presence of the female godhead in Judeo-Christianity.

What Martin-Gardner is able to achieve in *The Hidden Goddess* is no modest undertaking, but as an adept and impassioned writer dedicated to her craft and to facilitating candid, social discourse on modern spirituality, she stays the course in her exploration, undaunted by the disagreeable, if not outright ugly, truths that tend to make this subject matter unpalatable in devoutly religious circles. The goddess has never truly been hidden, after all. She's been here all along, albeit silent, but standing in plain sight, as if to say, "Your unwillingness to call me a goddess does not, cannot in fact, dethrone me."

As Martin-Gardner illustrates, the more history seems to push against the divine feminine, the stronger she ultimately becomes. Despite being perceived as a threat on nearly every level of society throughout the history of Judaism and Christianity, she has never sought to compete for the love of her people, dominate their faith, or attempt to overthrow her male counterpart, Yahweh. Simply put, the goddess has only wanted what women around the world have been fighting for over the course of thousands of years, equality.

In the quest for finding the Judeo-Christian goddess, if not liberating her presence from obscurity altogether, Martin-Gardner has brought into sharp relief that women's continuing struggle for equality has been a long and arduous road. As I write this here in the United States, those born at the beginning of this millennium have reached the age to vote, are on their way through college, or embarking on the next leg of their lives as adults for the very first time. Along with this new generation becoming productive and vocal parts of Western society, is the centennial anniversary of Women's Suffrage in the United States and a renewed focus on woman's rights, such as equal pay for equal work in employment and maternity leave, to name but two.

Women make up half of the population in the United States, yet they occupy less than ten percent of the seats in the Federal government's legislature. As we see in *The Hidden Goddess*, not much has changed. The goddess has been vying for equal power in the Judeo-Christian pantheon since its inception. Furthermore, Martin-Gardner's exploration into ancient history, going back nearly six thousand years, reveals the turbulent social climate and politics that incited religious sparring matches between kings, clerics and prophets that aren't too unlike the clashes between modern-day cults of personality.

We have ultimately arrived at a tale that will sound all too familiar, the tale of a deposed queen seeking to reclaim her throne. She has outlived the ancient leaders that have now turned to dust, religious leaders and pundits that vaingloriously persecuted her and sought her ruination if they couldn't simply silence her. In denying her a title or place at the altar, they wiped her from the minds of her people. In demonizing her iconography, they wiped her from their hearts. What were once her blessings of comfort—the promise of reincarnation (childbirth) and her mothering "Nature" (the sacred tree)—were now deemed as punishments or sources thereof. Even the female body, once a symbol of life and miracles, was relegated to being a mere piece of clay pottery, a vessel used only for carrying a child, nothing more.

This campaign against the goddess would endure the ages and serve as the very foundation of worldwide persecution against women in the modern era. But *The Hidden Goddess* illustrates the patience and grace of the indomitable sacred feminine. She inspires in her persistence and tenacity, ever steadfast in her quiet campaign as a reigning symbol of validation to all women, as well as their rightful, autonomous representation in the temples and the heavens.

Chantel Lysette is a researcher and consultant in the fields of spirituality and the paranormal, with a focus on comparative religion and the divine feminine. She has authored several books, such as her anecdotal *Angelic Pathways*, which has been printed around the world in multiple languages. She has enjoyed the success of her lecture series, both live and online.

Chapter One

The Quest

The Hidden Goddess. The banished and shattered goddess. The lost. The forgotten. Who was she? Who praised her name? And what fate befell her?

There are no easy answers to these questions. Details have been erased and distorted over the centuries. Her altars have been toppled and her sanctuaries razed. She is cloaked in controversy, welcomed by few and opposed by many. Yet despite the desperate attempts by reformers and zealots to erase her name from the collective human memory, remnants of her reign lingers, waiting to be discovered in the most unlikely of places – the Hebrew Bible.

To understand her story, we must for a moment, go back to the beginning. Although scholars now date the earliest examples of goddess worship to approximately 25,000 years ago, our story began in the second millennium BCE. Great civilizations had emerged along the Euphrates and Nile rivers. All-powerful kings and pharaohs shaped the destiny of humankind. Empires rose and fell, combined and dispersed.

For the common people of the era, survival was oftentimes incredibly difficult. Political turmoil, devastating poverty, and anxiety over the mysteries and danger that seemed to lurk around every corner permeated all aspects of life. The world was, as it had always been, in the midst of great change and evolution. To interpret the chaotic environment in which they lived, to glean from the unknown some sense of direction, the people of antiquity turned their thoughts to the higher realms of the gods and goddesses.

Just as their ancestors before them, the people of the ancient Near East recognized the divinity of the natural world. They looked down at their feet and saw grass and grain sprout forth and saw the goddesses of life and fertility. They looked up at the gathering clouds and saw the familiar face of the sky gods and life-bringing storm gods. They felt the celestial in every breath of wind, every cry of a newborn child, and every turn of the seasons. Throughout the entire ancient world, men and women searched for meaning beyond themselves and found a host of gods and goddesses gazing back at them.

A myriad of vibrant and beautiful mythologies sprang from the ancient person's search for the divine. Every aspect of life and death was controlled by a ruling deity. Those beings worked together, and sometimes against each other, to control and guide the development of the cosmos and of civilizations. And although the details frequently varied between empires, some forces emerged again and again. Among the most beloved and ancient was the great Mother Goddess. Her name would change, her realm would grow and shrink, but for thousands of years her importance stood as a testimony to her worth and power.[1]

The significance of goddess worship in the ancient world cannot be overstated. Men and women alike looked to the comfort of the Mother Goddess and petitioned her for blessings of love and progeny. Her role in the universe often reflected the role of mortal women. She was a mother, wife, daughter, and sister. She oversaw the fruits of agriculture, ran the household, and healed the sick and injured. From her body sprang not only children but the earth itself. She was the foundation of the faith of millions. Recognizing the duality of nature and the need for both male and female energies, the Mother Goddess stood as an equal to the Father God for millennia.

But in a rather unremarkable corner of the Near East, the idea of One True God had begun to grow. A small group of people were about to step off the well-worn paths of their ancestors and begin their own extraordinary journey. It was a journey that would, quite literally, change the course of humanity forever.

Scholars and theologians have long debated the exact details of the founding of Israel and its radical monotheistic ideals. The historical truths have been lost to us through the centuries, due either to the simple passing of time or to the revising of history by a host of Biblical authors often writing hundreds of years after the events they recorded. However, the Pentateuch (or first five books of the Hebrew Bible) provide an account of the forming of the Israelite nation as the people themselves believed it to have occurred.

Once slaves in the land of Egypt, Moses, the prophet of the god Yahweh, had delivered the people from their bonds in an epic known simply as the Exodus. After their miraculous escape, the people wandered in the wilderness until finally they came to the base of Mt. Sinai. Descending on the mountain as fire and smoke[2] Yahweh revealed himself to Moses and the assembly of fearful, awe-struck people and delivered his laws and commandments for his newly amassed followers. Moses and Yahweh then formed a covenant declaring, among other things, that "thou shalt have no other gods before me,"[3] and the foundations were laid for the three great monotheistic religions we know today – Judaism, Christianity, and Islam.

Up until this moment in history, the earth and heavens had been filled with a host of gods, goddesses, and other powerful divine creatures. Their existence was unquestioned. The very cycles of life were set into motion by the divinities. Yahweh, however, sought to dethrone these other supreme beings and set himself apart and above them. This was a profound shift in the dynamics of the cosmos. Within polytheistic religions, there had always been room for another god. Conquered nations often blended their own deities with those of their new masters and vice versa. Some gods and goddesses were so powerful that their influence stretched across many nations and throughout hundreds of years.[4] From this constant melding of people and ideals, new beliefs flourished and religious tolerance was natural. No one god or goddess set out to claim superiority. But Yahweh, the god of Israel, had declared himself King, above the reproach of man or god.

Despite what some Biblical adherents would like us to believe, the Israelite people did not spring from the dark ages of paganism fully formed and faithful to no god but Yahweh. Instead, they shared many of the same beliefs as their contemporaries in Mesopotamia, Egypt, and Canaan.[5] Moses may have agreed to have no god before Yahweh, but it was a promise that his people often found difficult to abide by. Exodus 32 tells us that even before Moses came down from Mt. Sinai, his people had cast a calf of gold to worship and give thanks to for their liberation from Egypt. Monotheism was a new and difficult concept to grasp, and the reign of the gods and goddesses would not easily be deposed.

Although the Bible is clear that Yahweh transcends the bounds of gender, that his form is unknowable and crafted of pure spirit, he is unmistakably male in his depictions. The Hebrew language, the original language of the Bible, assigns a gender to every noun, pronoun, verb, and adjective. Without fail, the words used to describe Yahweh are unquestionably male. As Raphael Patai wrote in his groundbreaking work, *The Hebrew Goddess*, "Every verbal statement about God conveyed the idea that He was male." And no efforts were ever made to alter that perspective. Yahweh did not need a physical body to be perceived as masculine. It was undeniably present in everything he did.

To some extent, Yahweh's maleness was irrelevant. He simply absorbed the powers and characteristics of his rival gods. This was a normal and familiar step in the progression of polytheistic faiths. Gods absorbed and fused with other deities all the time. For the early Hebrews, Yahweh didn't seem much different than the Canaanite gods El or Baal. In fact, there is a substantial amount of evidence suggesting that the God of the earliest sections of the Hebrew Bible did not represent Yahweh at all. Instead, it is most likely El, the father of humankind and gods alike, that is speaking to the patriarch Abraham in the book of Genesis.[6] Yahweh undoubtedly filled the role of the father god for the Hebrews just as El had done for the Canaanite people. But Yahweh did not stop with the conquest of the gods. He was the One and Only. And there was no room for the goddess in his heaven or earth.

Unfortunately for Yahweh, and the early champions of monotheism, the goddess would not easily be conquered. She would not relent her powers quietly to this new entity, and her followers would not cast her aside. The overarching maleness of Yahweh left a gaping void in the hearts of the people where once the Divine Feminine in all her incarnations had resided. No longer was there a Great Mother to nurture and guide her children. No longer did women appear as an equal, complementary figure to men. Men were firmly in control of heaven, and below on earth, the patriarchy of the Hebrews was soundly in place. They corrupted the goddess' names, razed her groves, smashed her altars, and defaced her icons. And yet, she persisted.

Scholars now understand that the Hebrew people worshiped a multitude of deities, especially the goddess in her various manifestations.[7] This, of course, was utterly scandalous when the evidence first began appearing and even today is vehemently denied by many of the faithful. But a careful reading of the Bible, especially the Old Testament, reveals that not only did the people retain parts of their pagan leanings, but that often these beliefs and practices fused with their worship of Yahweh. Especially among the common people (who formed the vast majority of the Hebrew nation), paganism blended with the One True God to form a plethora of varieties and flavors of Yahwism. And many of those focused on the goddess who filled the chasm left in a universe ruled solely by the masculine.

Verse after verse in the Bible describes the early church

leaders and rulers relentlessly trying to annihilate the worship of other deities. Often, they appear to succeed. That is, until the next generation of Hebrews came into power and restored the ancient practices. It was a battle that was repeated again and again throughout the Bible.

Eventually, Yahweh did prove victorious over the ancient pagan gods. The old beliefs had been twisted and perverted in such a way that the faithful began to fear the paths of their ancestors. The old gods seemed foreign and the goddess an abomination. Monotheism and patriarchy took firm control over the course of humanity, for better or for worse. The goddess had finally been destroyed, her domain fully assimilated by Yahweh.

Or was she?

Perhaps there is something in human nature that yearns for a great mother figure. Carl Jung, father of analytical psychology, certainly believed so. He saw the Mother Goddess as an archetypal figure, always at work in the human psyche.[8] Archaeological evidence has shown that it was the goddess that first appeared when man turned his thoughts to higher realms. For thousands of years she had tread among her children, mortal and god alike. Yahwism did, undeniably, a thorough job of extinguishing her hold on the hearts of man. But her seeds had already been planted. We see her shadow throughout the Bible and in the material remains of a people whose beginnings now lie in mystery and myth. She is there still, awaiting rediscovery – hidden, but not dead.

This book seeks to breathe life back in to the goddesses of the Hebrew faiths. The Divine Feminine remains, buried among the pages of countless authors, in many subtle ways. She first emerges as the unknown wife of God before being thoroughly dismantled within the Garden of Eden. And although her destruction was almost certain, she rises again as light and glory before birthing the child of God. She fills the spirit of the powerful and rebellious. Her symbols stand within Paradise and the Temple of Jerusalem. Her names may have been forgotten, but her presence still lingers.

This is the quest to find the Divine Feminine long lost within the Hebrew faiths. This is the story of the Hidden Goddess.

Chapter Two

The Queen

Upon each hilltop, among rings of standing stones and simple wooden poles, they placed their altars. The sweet smell of incense drifted among them, carrying their prayers heavenward. Others gathered beneath the trees, finding solace among the rustling of the green leaves. Across the land, families placed lovingly made clay effigies in their homes with the hope that they would bring fertility and abundance. The children of Israel lifted their heads and called her name – Asherah.

The story of the Hidden Goddess begins in the ancient Canaanite city of Ugarit in present day Syria. It was there, in 1928, that an accidental discovery would challenge everything scholars presumed to know about the birth of the Hebrew faith. While plowing an unremarkable field, a farmer chanced upon an ancient tomb in a forgotten necropolis. Over the next seven decades, archaeologists would uncover a city whose beginnings date back as far as 6000 BCE. Within the city, a treasure trove of cuneiform tablets began to reveal the rich mythology of the Ugaritic people. It was within these fragile tablets that the lost goddess Asherah was rediscovered and introduced to the modern world.[1]

In the Ugaritic tales she is known as Athirat and is the consort to the great father god, El. Multiple inscriptions tell us that her domain was the sea and all its abundance. As the "creatress of the gods," she birthed the Canaanite pantheon and served as wet nurse to the gods. She was also known to favor worthy mortals and is often portrayed as a mediator between her husband and those that would seek his favor. She was known to be both wise and kind, possessing the gift of foresight which she used to guide her mortal and immortal children. Over time, she claimed the role of fertility goddess, aiding the Canaanite women during the precarious days of pregnancy and childbirth.[2]

Further evidence reveals that Athirat's influence stretched far beyond Ugarit and even Canaan itself. In Sumerian documents dating from approximately 1750 BCE (a full three centuries before the majority of the Ugaritic documents were written), she is referred to as Ashratum, the bride of Anu (El). We find her in Southern Arabia, and in the Amarna tablets from Egypt. Often, the manifestation of the goddess was particular to a specific location. She is both the Asherah of Tyre and the Elath of Sidon, ancient Phoenician port cities in present day Lebanon that depended on the favor of "the lady of the sea."[3]

By the time the Hebrews entered into Canaan after their long sojourn in the desert, worship of Athirat was already well established. Although Moses had made a covenant between Yahweh and the Hebrews, the vast majority of the people were happy to cling to the old gods and customs just as their ancestors had done. In Athirat, they found a loving and nurturing mother, very different from the distant and often angry Yahweh. And, as it had happened countless times before, Athirat evolved among her new children and the Hebrew goddess Asherah was born.

The discovery of the Ugaritic tablets was, of course, immediately controversial. Scholars had long believed that the Biblical account of the founding of monotheism was an accurate record of historical events. The Hebrew faith had been declared superior to that of the dangerous pagan ways of the past. Yahweh had emerged separately, in the earliest days of the patriarchs, and declared himself the One and Only. Who then was this goddess among the people of Israel? And what did her presence tell us about the foundations of the three great monotheistic religions of the world?

It is quite easy today, in a world ruled by monotheistic faiths, to forget that the foundations of those religions sprang from a world teeming with gods and goddesses. We now know that much of the Bible was written decades (or in some cases, centuries) after the events it records. By that time, monotheism was well on its way to dominance, and the writers could mold the stories in a way that reflected their own beliefs. The Hebrews had not always been monotheistic, but the authors of the Bible wanted them to appear as such. Hints of other deities and beliefs among the people were often downplayed, manipulated, or outright ignored. Yahwistic monotheism may have been the ideal, but it would take centuries for it to be fully realized and accepted among the Hebrews.

After the discovery of the texts in Ugarit, some scholars began to reexamine the accepted facts about the development of the Hebrew faith. Upon doing so, they began to uncover multiple accounts of the goddess hidden in plain sight within the Old Testament. Her story began to emerge as misinterpreted passages were read correctly for the first time in millennia. Suddenly, stories that had once seemed out of place or incomplete, made sense in the context of polytheistic Israel. Although it can be difficult to find in modern English translations of the Bible, Asherah appears some forty times within the Old Testament. And often, what we *aren't* told is just as important as what is recorded.

One of the earliest mentions of Asherah takes place in the Book of Judges. In Judges 6:25 Yahweh speaks to a man named Gideon, telling him "tear down your father's altar to Baal and cut down the Asherah pole beside it." Fearing the wrath of the men of the city, Gideon waited until dark to carry out the Lord's order. The next morning, when the destruction was discovered, the men demanded to know who had committed the heinous crime. When they discovered it was Gideon, they marched to his father's house and demanded, "Bring out your son. He must die, because he has broken down Baal's altar and cut down the Asherah pole beside it."[4] It is only through the intercession of Joash, Gideon's father and chieftain, that his life was spared.

This event, although quite brief, reveals much about the polytheistic practices of the Hebrew people. Throughout the Old Testament, Baal the Canaanite storm god, takes center stage in the fight for the hearts of the Hebrews. Originally the son of Athirat (Asherah) and El, the cult of Baal was already well established throughout Canaan when the Hebrews arrived. Like the worship of Asherah, Baal was readily embraced by the people. For several hundred years, Baal would be at the heart of the battle between the polytheistic past and the monotheistic future. Most often, Asherah can be found in context with Baal.

The text clearly states that the altar and Asherah pole belonged to Joash, Gideon's father. Asherah poles, although time and weather conditions have eradicated any archaeological trace of them, are understood to have been wooden poles erected in honor of the goddess.[5] From her earliest incarnations, Asherah was always associated with trees and sacred groves. Asherah poles may have been a stylized image of the goddess herself or fashioned to look like a living tree. It's also possible that groups of these poles were used to form a sacred grove of sorts when living trees were not present. Most often though, Asherah poles were placed next to altars in a bid to honor and evoke the goddess. Joash, having erected both an altar to Baal and an Asherah pole, was quite possibly a priest of both. At the very least, he was a proponent of their cults and had created a communal space for them within his city where his people could gather to worship the deities.

The altar and pole were certainly very important to Joash's people as they demanded nothing less than Gideon's life for their destruction. The Hebrews were devoted to Baal and Asherah, and they would not relinquish their beliefs easily. Unfortunately, this clash with Gideon was simply a precursor to what would follow. It would be several generations before another Yahwistic reformer would challenge the authority of the god and goddess, but the war against polytheism had only just begun.

Although Asherah's Biblical story doesn't pick up again until the Book of 1 Kings, her worship remained an integral part of the lives of the common Hebrew. Her presence was so ingrained into the cultural landscape, that most would have seen her as a necessary aspect of daily life. Each time a child was born, she was celebrated. Every bountiful harvest of fish or grain, she was thanked. For the common people, her role as the loving mother goddess was much more accessible than the remote father god Yahweh. In the beginning, worship of Asherah was largely a communal affair practiced primarily among the rural Hebrew people. But although her story retreated into the background for a while, her influence continued to grow and would eventually permeate the loftiest of halls and the holiest of sanctuaries.

Around the year 970 BCE, Solomon, son of the revered King David, took the throne in Israel. Just before his death, David had charged Solomon with obedience to Yahweh saying, "Observe what the Lord your God requires: walk in obedience to him, and keep his decrees and commands, his laws and regulations as written in the Law of Moses."[6] As a reward for abiding by his laws, Yahweh had promised that the line of David would endure forever. Solomon readily agreed and pledged to obey the covenant made with his father's God. He quickly discovered, however, that obedience to Yahweh's staunch decrees would not be easy. The Biblical writers record, "Solomon showed his love for the Lord by walking according to the instructions given him by his father David, except that he offered sacrifices and burned incense on the high places."[7] Solomon even visited Gibeon, the "most important high place" and offered a thousand burnt sacrifices. Afterwards, Yahweh appeared to Solomon and granted him the gift of wisdom to rule over his people fairly.

But to whom did Solomon make his sacrifices to in the high places? The Biblical writers saw this act as a transgression against Yahweh, but afterwards Yahweh seemingly rewarded Solomon for his actions. Not only did he grant Solomon wisdom and discernment, he blessed him with riches and honor. The Bible is full of contradictions, but this one seems quite telling when compared to what many modern scholars now believe. It was to Asherah, the *wife* of Yahweh, that Solomon made his offerings.

Undoubtedly, stating that the One and Only God of Israel once had a wife or consort is nothing short of blasphemous in the eyes of many of the faithful. The idea has been vehemently denied since the first group of scholars dared to broach the subject. It wasn't until a discovery in the mid-1970s that mainstream Biblical scholars began to take a closer look at the relationship between Yahweh and Asherah. It was then, at the site of Kuntillat Ajrud in the northeast Sinai, that two large storage jars known as *pithoi* were discovered. While these types of jars are relatively common, it was the inscriptions that caught the attention of the archaeologists. One read, "Amaryau said to my lord...may you be blessed by Yahweh and by his Asherah." Another inscription from the same site read, "I have blessed you by Yahweh...and his Asherah." Nine miles away at a site west of Hebron, another inscription was uncovered that read, "Uriah the rich has caused it to be written: Blessed be Uriah by Yahweh and by his Asherah; from his enemies he has saved him."[8] But what exactly do these inscriptions imply?

As it often happens with controversial topics, researchers interpret the discoveries differently. Some argue that the Asherah referred to in the inscriptions are nothing more than wooden poles, ignoring that the poles are themselves representations of the goddess. Even if the inscriptions reference nothing more than a cultic item known as an Asherah, they still connect the goddess to the worship of Yahweh. And they place her in a very interesting position.

Throughout the ancient world, gods and goddesses had always been paired into couples. The Ugaritic texts tell us that Athirat, an early incarnation of Asherah, was the consort of the god El. Yahweh absorbed many of El's aspects as he usurped the traditional pantheon. Is it so difficult to believe that he would also take El's bride for his own? For the people of ancient Israel, steeped in the world of polytheism, it would have been completely natural for Yahweh to be paired with a female deity. There can be little doubt that it was Asherah that the people chose to reign next to their God.

Fulfilling one of Yahweh's earlier promises to David, in the fourth year of his reign Solomon began construction of a grand temple in Jerusalem. When it was completed seven years later, Solomon dedicated the temple to Yahweh, declaring him superior to all other gods in heaven or on earth.[9] Yahweh repeatedly reminded Solomon of the provisions of his agreement with David – as long as Solomon and his people remained dedicated to him, he would provide for and protect them forever.

Solomon, however, chose many of his wives from other nations, an act expressly forbidden by Yahweh in fear that "they will surely turn your hearts after their gods."[10] Ignoring this warning, Solomon honored his wives by building temples to their native deities throughout Jerusalem. "As Solomon grew old, his wives turned his heart after other gods, and his heart was not fully devoted to the Lord his God, as the heart of David his father had been."[11] By building and dedicating these temples, it was Solomon himself that brought the worship of Asherah out of the countryside and into the capital city of Jerusalem.

Solomon's devotion to other deities greatly angered Yahweh. In his rage he promised to tear the kingdom from Solomon's hand and deliver it to one of his servants. He raised enemies to move against Israel, including one of Solomon's own officials, Jeroboam. Speaking through the prophet Ahijah of Shiloh, Yahweh promised Jeroboam "you will rule over all that your heart desires; you will be king over Israel."[12] Jeroboam was also warned, just as Solomon had been, that he must keep the commandments of Yahweh if he desired a lasting monarchy. Solomon attempted to have Jeroboam killed, but he fled to Egypt and remained there until the king died around 931 BCE.

Solomon's death marked the end of a unified Israel. Just as Yahweh had warned Solomon, part of the country was torn from his son and successor, Rehoboam. Refusing to accept Rehoboam's harsh rule, the northern tribes fulfilled Ahijah's prophecy and named Jeroboam king of Israel. Rehoboam was left to rule the smaller and newly formed nation of Judah. And although both nations had been commanded to serve no other god but Yahweh, worship of the goddess Asherah continued to grow. Her influence would infiltrate palaces and temples alike and would be at the center of some of the most intriguing events recorded in the Old Testament.

Just as his father before him, Rehoboam found it difficult to turn away from the ancient customs of his ancestors. The Biblical authors recorded, "Judah did evil in the eyes of the Lord. By the sins they committed they stirred up his jealous anger more than those who were before them had done. They also set up for themselves high places, sacred stones, and Asherah poles on every high hill and under every spreading tree."[13] Maacah, Rehoboam's favorite wife, was a devoted follower of the mother goddess. Under her influence, the worship of Asherah infiltrated the holiest of all places – Solomon's Temple.

Asherah's statue stood at the altar of Yahweh, within the Temple of Jerusalem, throughout Rehoboam's reign. It remained in its place of honor throughout the short reign of his son, Abijah, as well. However, when Asa took the throne after the death of Abijah, Judah experienced its first Yahwistic reform. Asa diligently followed the laws given to the Hebrews by Yahweh: "He removed the foreign altars and the high places, smashed the sacred stones and cut down the Asherah poles. He commanded Judah to seek the Lord, the God of their ancestors, and to obey his laws and commands. He removed the high places and incense altars in every town in Judah, and the kingdom was at peace under him."[14] He also stripped Maacah of the power she had exerted over Rehoboam and Abijah "because she had made a repulsive image for the worship of Asherah."[15] It is recorded that Asa himself removed the statue from the Temple and burned it in the Kidron Valley.

Asa's extensive reforms, including the deposing of Maacah, are recorded in both the book of 1 Kings and 2 Chronicles. In each book, directly following the account of Asa removing the Asherah from the Temple, the Biblical authors add, "Although he did not remove the high places, Asa's heart was fully committed to the Lord all his life".[16] This is, of course, a direct contradiction to the verse that describes the destruction of the high places.[17] How do we account for this discrepancy? How could Asa do what was right in the eyes of Yahweh without destroying the high places associated with worship of the goddess Asherah?

Asa's heart may have belonged to Yahweh alone, but the people of Judah did not share his monotheistic convictions. As soon as one shrine or altar fell, another took its place. The people clung to their goddess, resurrecting her each time she was cut down. Asa may have removed Asherah from the Temple, but he could not remove her from the hearts of the Judeans. And oddly, the Biblical writers don't seem overly concerned with the actions of the people or that Asa did not remove the high places permanently from Judah. He is still considered a good and faithful king that ruled his people in accordance to Yahweh's laws. Perhaps this is because the worship of Asherah was seen, at least among the majority of Judeans, as complementary to the worship of Yahweh. Some may have even seen the worship of Asherah as an essential, balancing part of Yahwism.

Just as in Judah, Asherah worship continued under Jeroboam's reign in Israel as well. Yahweh, speaking through the prophet Ahijah, had promised Jeroboam that he would rule over all his heart desired[18] as long as he walked in obedience and in accordance to the Lord's decrees. But Jeroboam feared that his people would make pilgrimages to the Temple in Jerusalem and thus be swayed to abandon Israel for Judah. To prevent this, Jeroboam set up two golden calves and said to his people, "It is too much for you to go up to Jerusalem. Here are your gods, Israel, who brought you up out of Egypt."[19] He then built new shrines in the high places and appointed priests (including himself) to them. And where there was an altar on a high place, the goddess Asherah was present.

Although Asherah isn't mentioned specifically, the Bible tells us that Jeroboam's successors walked in his sinful ways and angered Yahweh. We can infer from these brief passages that worship of the goddess continued, unhindered and unaffected by the Yahwistic reform taking place in Judah under Asa and his heir, Jehoshaphat. With the reign of Ahab in Israel, however, Asherah returned to center stage in a remarkable showdown with one of the Bible's most enigmatic figures.

Once again, it would be the favorite wife of the king, this time a Sidonian princess that helped propel worship of Asherah into Israel's capital city of Samaria. Her name was Jezebel, wife of Ahab and daughter of Ethbaal the king of Sidon. In Sidon, worship of Elath (Asherah) was an ancient and well-established norm, dating back at least five hundred years before the birth of Jezebel. To strengthen Israel's alliance with Sidon, and in an effort to please his wife, Ahab "set up an altar for Baal in the temple of Baal that he built in Samaria," and he "also made an Asherah pole and did more to arouse the anger of the Lord, the God of Israel, than did all the kings of Israel before him."[20]

Disgusted and outraged by the apparent sinfulness of Ahab and the false gods of Jezebel, the prophet Elijah set out to prove that Yahweh alone was the God of Israel. Elijah issued a challenge to Ahab, demanding that he "summon the people from all over Israel to meet me on Mount Carmel. And bring the four hundred and fifty prophets of Baal and the four hundred prophets of Asherah, who eat at Jezebel's table."[21] Once assembled, Elijah set out the rules for his challenge: "Get two bulls for us. Let Baal's prophets choose one for themselves, and let them cut it into pieces and put it on the wood but not set fire to it. I will prepare the other bull and put it on the wood but not set fire to it. Then you call on the name of your god, and I will call on the name of the Lord. The god who answers by fire – he is God."[22]

As expected, Elijah is triumphant in his challenge. Baal did not answer the calls of his priests, but Yahweh easily and dramatically lit the fire of sacrifice, despite the water Elijah had ordered poured over the altar. Having witnessed this awesome display of dominance, the people of Israel fell to their knees and proclaimed Yahweh as God. Elijah then ordered that the prophets of Baal, all 450 of them, be taken into the Kishon Valley and slaughtered.

But what of the 400 prophets of Asherah also called to the confrontation of gods at Mount Carmel? Incredibly, there is no record of what befell Asherah's faithful. Elijah ensured that each and every priest of Baal was executed, but it would seem that Asherah's priests were spared. Why would Elijah, a staunch Yahwist reformer, allow the worship of a pagan goddess to continue after his awe-inspiring defeat of Baal?

As with many of the reformers throughout the Hebrew Bible, Elijah's focus was on the destruction of the cult of Baal, the rival of Yahweh. It was Baal that threatened to usurp Yahweh's prominence and therefore, had to be stopped. But Asherah was not Yahweh's rival, nor was she perceived as a threat to Yahwists. Perhaps it was because Asherah was viewed as an inevitable counterpart to the Lord of the Hebrews. She quietly established the balance of male and female power in heaven. Elijah may not have approved of her existence, but he certainly appeared tolerant of her presence among the Israelites. Because they were not slaughtered along the banks of the Kishon with the priests of Baal, we can assume that Asherah's prophets were allowed to continue their devotion to the goddess even as Elijah worked to bring Israel back to Yahweh.

As the epic clash between Elijah and the priests was happening in Israel, in Judah, Asa's son Jehoshaphat continued the work that his father had begun. It is recorded in 2 Chronicles 19:3 that Jehoshaphat had removed the Asherahs from the countryside once again. Although Asa had attempted to rid Judah of the goddess already, her faithful were persistent. When one sacred grove was destroyed, another was planted. For every Asherah pole felled, one stood ready to take its place.

Ten years after the death of Jehoshaphat, the cult of Asherah still flourished in Judah. It was around that time that the seven year old Joash became king of Israel. Under the tutelage of the priest Jehoiada, Joash "did what was right in the eyes of the Lord,"[23] which included the restoration of the Temple at Jerusalem. But things quickly changed after the death of Jehoiada. Joash, just like his forefathers, had not removed the high places from Judah.[24] With Jehoiada gone, Joash called an assembly of his officials from throughout the land. They implored him to restore the ancient religions, and with Joash's blessing "they abandoned the temple of the Lord, the God of their ancestors, and worshiped Asherah poles and idols."[25] Under Joash the statue of Asherah was restored to the inner sanctuary of the Temple. For the next hundred years, she would stand undisturbed at the altar of Yahweh.

While Joash reigned in Judah, Jehohaz took the throne in the kingdom of Israel. Jehohaz, as so many kings before him, "did evil in the eyes of the Lord."[26] And although Jehohaz did petition Yahweh for help against the oppression of Israel by Hazeal, king of Aram, "they did not turn away from the sins of the house of Jeroboam, which he had caused Israel to commit; they continued in them. Also, the Asherah pole remained standing in Samaria."[27].

By the time of Jehohaz, the cult of Baal in Israel had been effectively defeated. A terrible and thorough massacre of the priests of Baal had occurred under Jehu, Jehohaz's father. But once again, there is no mention of a similar fate among the priests of Asherah. And if, as the Bible clearly states, the Asherah pole still stood in Samaria under Jehohaz, it is safe to assume that the cult of Asherah persevered. Asherah remained an important and revered goddess, openly worshiped among both the common people and the royal court, until the Kingdom of Israel was conquered in 720 BCE by the Neo-Assyrian Empire.[28]

As the northern kingdom of Israel was coming to an end, a zealous Yahwist reformer was taking the throne in Judah. Hezekiah, doing what was right in the eyes of the Lord, "removed the high places, smashed the sacred stones and cut down the Asherah poles."[29] He also ordered the cleansing and consecration of the Temple of Solomon, including the removal of "all defilement from the sanctuary."[30] At Hezekiah's bidding, after decades of standing next to the altar of Yahweh, the statue of Asherah was removed from the inner temple. Taking it and the golden serpent cast by Moses, the priests disposed of them in the Kidron Valley. For his actions, the Biblical writers record that "there was no one like him (Hezekiah) among all the kings of Judah, either before him or after him"[31] and that "he was successful in whatever he undertook."[32]

Although Hezekiah followed the word of the God of Israel faithfully throughout the entirety of his life, his people still found it difficult to relinquish their fate to a single god. Despite Hezekiah's reforms, and even though the prophets Isaiah and Micah vigorously decried the cult of Asherah, the majority of Judeans held fast to their ancient practices.

Almost immediately after the death of Hezekiah, his son and successor, Manasseh, set about to restore all that his father's reforms had destroyed. He "rebuilt the high places his father Hezekiah had demolished; he also erected altars to Baal and made Asherah poles."[33] It was during this time that Asherah was once again placed in the Temple of Jerusalem, returned to her place of honor next to the altar of Yahweh.[34] There she remained until another Yahwist reformer, Josiah, took the throne in 640 BCE.

In the 18th year of Josiah's reign, a discovery heralded the end of polytheism among the people of Judah. Asherah had survived Ahab, Elijah, Jehu, and Hezekiah. But the newly found Book of Deuteronomy and its fanatical adherents would prove to be much more difficult to overcome. Ordering the complete destruction of all of the nations that inhabited Canaan, Deuteronomy also proclaimed: "Destroy completely all the places on the high mountains, on the hills and under every spreading tree, where the nations you are dispossessing worship their gods. Break down their altars, smash their sacred stones and burn their Asherah poles in the fire; cut down the idols of their gods and wipe out their names from those places."[35]

Just as Hezekiah had done, Josiah ordered the consecration of the Jerusalem Temple. He ordered the priests to "remove from the temple of the Lord all the articles made for Baal and Asherah and all the starry hosts."[36] Taking them again to the Kidron Valley, Josiah burnt all that was removed from the temple. The ashes he gathered up and had them carried to Beth-el, a place long associated with idolatrous worship. Next, he removed the Asherah pole itself from the inner temple, burnt it in the valley, and ground it to powder. He then, for reasons unknown, took the ashes and scattered them over the graves of those that had worshiped the goddess.[37] Finally, "he also tore down the quarters of the male shrine prostitutes that were in the temple of the Lord, and the quarters where women did weaving for Asherah."[38]

Josiah's brutal suppression of polytheism did not stop with the purging of the Temple. He then went out into the countryside, destroying and desecrating the sacred sites and high places, including the Temple of Ashtoreth built by Solomon. The Bible records that "Josiah smashed the sacred stones and cut down the Asherah poles and covered the sites with human bones."[39] He then turned his sight onto the high place created by Jeroboam, destroying the altar, burning the Asherah, and even defiling the tombs of the dead.

Spurred on by the words of Deuteronomy, Josiah did more than any other king before him to quell the power of the ancient deities. His wrath was swift and thorough. But it was also fleeting. Josiah, like so many before him, had overlooked the power of the goddess Asherah. He failed to recognize the devotion of her followers or the blessings she bestowed on her people. He had destroyed her physical representations, but he had not abolished her spirit. Soon after Josiah's death, her people once again reclaimed what had been torn from them. For wherever a hill stood or a tree grew, the goddess Asherah was there.

But despite her tenacity, and the devotion of her faithful, the days of the goddess were numbered. Indeed, the days of Judah itself were coming to a close. Twenty two years after Josiah's death, Nebuchadnezzar of Babylon besieged Jerusalem and the kingdom of Judah fell. Many were forcibly relocated leaving much of the land desolate. After the destruction of the Temple and the Babylonian conquest, Asherah is only mentioned among the many sins that led to the fall of Israel and Judah. In some revisions and translations of the Bible, her name is not mentioned at all. She is downgraded to no more than a wooden pole without meaning or a pagan grove of trees without purpose.

Writing long after the events they describe, the Deuteronomists (the name given to the group of writers responsible for the books of Joshua, Judges, Samuel, Kings, and Jeremiah) simply buried the goddess among a host of generic offenses. It's possible that by the time the books were first written down, much of Asherah's worship and history had already been forgotten. But it is far more likely that the Deuteronomists simply did not want to draw attention to her more than was absolutely necessary. They purposely denied the reader any detail into the beliefs and practices of the common people of Israel and Judah. No rites of

Asherah were ever recorded, or it they were, none have survived. There is no description, other than the burning of incense that recounts the rituals that took place on the high places or beneath the green trees. But we know, beyond any reasonable doubt, that the people clung to the goddess Asherah. When the Hebrews crossed into Canaan after their long sojourn in the desert, Asherah had been waiting on them. And she remained with them throughout the Babylonian destruction of Jerusalem and beyond.

Raphael Patai, in *The Hebrew Goddess*, sums up Asherah's presence beautifully: "Of the 370 years during which the Solomonic Temple stood in Jerusalem, for no less than 236 years (or almost 2/3 of the time) the statue of Asherah was present in the Temple, and her worship was part of the legitimate religion approved and led by the king, the court, and the priesthood and opposed by only a few prophetic voices crying out against it at relatively long intervals." Asherah's worship permeated all aspects of life and survival for the Hebrews. It would have been difficult, if not impossible, for them to imagine existence without her. There is simply no other explanation for the perseverance of her influence even as Yahweh sought to amass all the power of the heavens for himself.

In the end, Yahweh won the battle for supremacy. And even though at no point was the *existence* of other deities denied, Yahweh was proclaimed the Almighty God. Asherah, and countless other deities, were buried beneath the weight of monotheism. There can be, however, little doubt about the immense importance she played in the lives of the average Hebrew. For six centuries, she was the doting mother of the Hebrews, watching over and guiding her children despite those that rose up against her. Although there is much still to learn and discover, Asherah speaks to us of a rich and vibrant past long forgotten. A past where, for a time, a powerful goddess stood next to the God of the Hebrews as his equal.

But this would not be the end for Asherah, for she would continue to move through the shadows of the Judeo-Christian faiths, reemerging in strange and surprising ways.

Chapter Three

The Genesis

Looking into the enraged eyes of Adam, she finally understood. He would never perceive her as his equal though they had been born of the same clay, molded by the will of God in His own image. But she would not be caged. Not even in Paradise. Defiance flared up within her as she brazenly called out the sacred name of God and fled from the Garden. There, at the edge of the sea, she waited and watched as God crafted a new wife for Adam. Lilith thought her weak, subservient, and pathetic. But Eve would soon make a bold choice that would alter the course of humanity forever.

"In the beginning, God created the heavens and the earth."[1] So begins, quite arguably, the most famous creation story ever written by human hand. It's a remarkably simple story, condensing the creation of the cosmos and all the intricacies of life into a span of only seven days. God, alone in the void, crafted the entirety of the macrocosm, set into motion the passage of time, and filled the earth with life by simply willing it into being. But his crowning achievement, the pinnacle of all creation, he saved for last.

For his final creation on the sixth day, God looked to himself. "So God created them in his own image, in the image of God he created them; male and female he created them."[2] To the newly formed humans, he gave dominion of the earth and all the life it contained. And on the seventh day, God rested, pleased with the work he had done.

By the end of the first chapter of Genesis, creation was complete. Man and woman ruled over the earth together. They had been formed, as the Hebrew Bible clearly proclaimed, together at the end of the sixth day. Why then is there another, distinctly different, account recorded in the very next chapter of

Genesis?

The creation story recorded in Genesis 2 begins with a barren, newly formed world. As God had not sent any rain, "no shrub had yet appeared on the earth and no plant had yet sprung up."[3] It was in that lifeless landscape that God "formed a man from the dust of the ground and breathed into his nostrils the breath of life."[4] In this account of creation, man was the first living being formed. And he was utterly alone.

To the east, along the banks of a great river, God planted a vast and bountiful garden. From the rich soil, trees emerged that "were pleasing to the eye and good for food."[5] God then placed the man in the garden as its caretaker and directed his attention to a particular tree standing proudly at the center of Eden. God commanded, "You are free to eat from any tree in the garden; but you must not eat from the tree of knowledge of good and evil, for when you eat from it you will certainly die."[6]

Seeing that it was not good for man to be alone, God next set out to create a suitable helper for Adam. Man's purpose, after all, was to protect and cultivate the Garden of Eden. Such a daunting task would require assistance. So God "formed out of the ground all the wild animals and all the birds in the sky."[7] He brought the creatures before Adam who gave each a name but found no appropriate companion among them.

After rejecting each animal presented to him, God caused Adam to fall into a deep sleep so that he might craft a proper mate for him. While Adam slept, God "took one of the man's ribs and then closed up the place with flesh. Then the Lord God made a woman from the rib he had taken out of the man, and he brought her to the man."[8] Seeing this woman upon awakening, Adam declared, "This is now bone of my bones and flesh of my flesh. She shall be called 'woman' for she was taken out of man."[9] No longer alone in paradise, Adam took the woman as his wife and welcomed her into the garden. And with her birth, creation was completed.

The discrepancies between the two creation stories of Genesis are easy to discern. In the first account, known today among scholars as the "Priestly" version, man and woman were created simultaneously on the sixth day. They emerge as equals and are given dominion of the entire earth. The second, or "Yahwistic," account reversed the process. Man was created before the first drops of rain fell. He was born out of the dust of the earth just as the creatures of field and sky were formed later. He was crafted as a worker and kept within the confines of the Garden of Eden. Woman, in this narrative, was little more than an afterthought. She was the only living being forged not from the earth but from a piece of another creature. Her sole purpose was to serve Adam, and in turn, the God that created him.

Today, most scholars agree that the two accounts of creation recorded in Genesis were written by vastly different groups separated by hundreds of years. The "Yahwistic" account of Genesis 2 is generally considered the older account having first been recorded during the reign of King Solomon by members of the Hebrew tribes. The "Priestly" version recorded in Genesis 1 developed some 500 years later probably among elite Jewish theologians. However, both accounts are believed to have been based on oral traditions passed down among the Hebrews for many generations.[10]

Regardless of when they were written or by whom, the inconsistencies between the two tales created a multitude of problems for the early rabbis studying the Torah (or first five books of the Hebrew Bible). As the sacred and literal word of God, the rabbis believed the Bible simply could not contradict itself. A new interpretation, or midrash, was needed to unite the stories into one cohesive and understandable narrative. What emerged was not one, but two, powerful goddess figures that would shape the course of humanity and define all of womankind.

To reconcile the dissonance in Genesis, the early Jewish

scholars chose to completely disregard the two separate descriptions of the creation of man. Instead, they deduced, woman alone had been created twice. But why? What had happened to the first woman, the one born together with Adam on the sixth day of creation? Who was she?

She was Lilith, the first wife of Adam, created from the dust of the earth as man's equal. But she was a wild, untameable woman who would rather live as a feared recluse in the wilderness than to bow to Adam's will. Refusing to lie beneath Adam, she fled the Garden of Eden and cemented her place in Jewish lore as a warning against all willful and rebellious women and foreign goddesses.

Although she would become one of the most powerful and enigmatic figures in all of Jewish lore, the story of Lilith, like that of Asherah, began long before the birth of the Hebrews. The earliest known mention of Lilith comes from the Mesopotamian tale "Gilgamesh and the Huluppu Tree." Dating from approximately 2000 BCE, the story opened with the Sumerian queen of heaven, Inanna, spying a beautiful huluppu (willow) tree on the banks of the Euphrates. Inanna was so struck by the magnificent tree that she plucked it from the banks and replanted it in her own sacred garden. Under her gentle care, the tree thrived and grew tall and strong.

Wishing to craft herself a new throne, Inanna went to gather the wood of the huluppu tree once it was fully mature. She found her plans thwarted, however, by a trio of dangerous creatures that had taken up residence within the tree. A great snake was coiled around the base of the tree while a Zu bird had placed its nest in the upper branches. And in the middle stood the home of Lilith, the "maid of desolation."[11]

Seeing that her tree had been seized by three evil beings, Inanna wept. Hearing her cries, Gilgamesh, the great Sumerian hero, donned his armor and went to the aid of the goddess. Using his mighty ax, Gilgamesh slaughtered the snake with ease.

Seeing this, the Zu-bird fled with its young into the mountains. Lilith, in fear for life, tore down her house and escaped into the wilderness. With the beasts vanquished, the huluppu tree was finally cut down and presented to Inanna for her throne.

By the time "Gilgamesh and the Huluppu Tree" was first written down, Lilith was already a well-established figure in Sumerian culture.[12] A masculine version of her name, Lillu, first appeared in 2400 BCE in the Sumerian King List. The divine father of Gilgamesh himself, Lillu was originally a primordial storm spirit. He would later be transformed, probably due to an etymological error, into a much darker entity. As his female counterpart, Lilitu (Lilith) would also undergo this metamorphosis. Together, Lillu and Lilitu stalked the night as the first of a unique class of demons – incubi and succubi. Appearing first in dreams, the demons would then engage in sexual acts with their unsuspecting captives in order to spawn demonic children and to slowly leech away the victim's life force.

The role of the frightful succubus would follow Lilith throughout her history and become one of the defining aspects of her personality. In Babylon, she would acquire another horrific trait from her association with the goddess Lamashtu. Described as a monstrous hybrid, Lamashtu plagued pregnant women and their newborn children. Particularly fond of stealing suckling infants, she would then slaughter the child in order to feast on the bones and blood of the innocent. Because she was often portrayed with similar physical attributes as Lilith, the role of child-slayer would eventually be attributed to Lilith as well.

Lilith emerged from the great Mesopotamian kingdoms not as a lowly she-demon, but as a terrible goddess to be feared and revered. Babylonian artifacts portrayed her as a beautiful woman whose long hair tumbled down her shapely body. Her earliest association with storms and wind had given her strong wings and the sharp talons of an owl. However, her beauty could not veil the heart of the demon that lay within her. Her presence was feared in every home and each time a newborn child died suddenly, her name was cursed. When she finally entered the Jewish mythos, much of the foundations of her story had already been laid.

After appearing only briefly in the Babylonian Talmud, a principal text of Rabbinic Judaism, one medieval text forever altered the tale of Lilith. It was within the anonymously written midrash *The Alphabet of Ben Sira* that the previously unnamed first wife of Adam finally received an identity.[13] Already one of the most feared demons among the Jewish people thanks to the dispersion of the Babylonian myths, Lilith was elevated to the woman of Genesis 1, crafted by the hand of God himself.

Why the author of *The Alphabet* chose the Mesopotamian Lilith as the first wife of Adam is unknown. Perhaps it was her wild and unruly nature that first drew his attention. To the faithful, the first female had been unworthy and rebellious. Lilith embodied everything that Israelite men feared in a woman – strength, power, and independence – and recalled the dangers of the Goddess.

Having been crafted in the same manner as Adam on the sixth day of creation, Lilith rightfully saw herself as man's equal. Adam, however, had a very different idea. Wishing to have sex with the alluring Lilith, Adam demanded that she lie beneath him. Lilith scoffed and inquired, "Why should I lie beneath you, when I am your equal, since both of us were created from dust?" Adam, enraged by her rejection, attempted to overpower Lilith and force himself on her. To escape, Lilith did the only thing within her power to do – she called out the Tetragrammaton, the ineffable name of God. Upon saying the sacred name, Lilith rose into the air and flew away to the edge of the Red Sea.

During the time of creation, the Red Sea was a desolate and evil place filled with a host of demonic spirits. No mention of their origins is offered, but they welcomed Lilith into their legion. Freed from the restraints of God and man, Lilith enjoyed unbridled promiscuity among the demons. From her affairs, she gave birth to a host of demonic spawn each day.

As Lilith reveled in her new found freedom, Adam brooded over his perceived insult. Adam begged God to return Lilith to him, and in answer to his plea, God sent three angels to find her. Senoy, Sansenoy, and Semangelof found her and demanded she return with them. But Lilith refused, even when the angels threatened to drown her for her disobedience. Her sole purpose for existing, she told the angels, was to weaken and slay infants. She claimed dominion over every male child from birth to eight days and over females for twenty days. When she saw that the angels were not swayed, she offered them a compromise. A deal was struck that each day one hundred of Lilith's demonic offspring would perish and that she would harm no child bearing an amulet inscribed with the names of the three angels sent to retrieve her.[14]

As God did not see it fit for Adam to remain alone after the angels failed to return with Lilith, he again crafted a woman to be Adam's helper. This woman, as recorded in Genesis 2, would not be formed in the same manner as Adam. She would not be man's equal for her very existence depended on the rib removed from Adam's side.

While Lilith enjoyed her wild escapade among the demons, the demure second woman (who had not yet received a name) spent her days amid the tall trees and creeping vines of the Garden of Eden. Creatures great and small shared Paradise with her and Adam, including the serpent who "was more crafty than any of the wild animals the Lord God had made". One day, the serpent approached Eve and inquired, "Did God really say, 'You must not eat from any tree in the garden'?"[15] Eve answered, repeating what Adam had told to her as God had not spoken to her since her birth, "We may eat fruit from the trees in the garden, but God did say, 'You must not eat fruit from the tree that is in the middle of the garden, and you must not touch it, or you will die'."[16]

Dismissing the warning of God, the serpent assured the woman that eating of the Tree of Knowledge would not lead to death but to greater understanding. The serpent promised, "For God knows that when you eat from it your eyes will be opened, and you will be like God, knowing good and evil."[17] The woman gazed up at the tree, and indeed it did appear good for food. But it was not fruit alone that she craved. Food was plentiful in the Garden of Eden. Knowledge, however, was limited. God had never even spoken to the woman, and he certainly had not shared knowledge with her. Perhaps she believed that eating of the Tree would be the only opportunity she'd ever have for acquiring something more than she'd been given.

As the woman reached out to pluck the fruit, Adam watched. He had been present for the entire exchange between the woman and the serpent. At no point had he intervened, corrected the serpent, or demanded that the woman not eat the fruit. Instead, "she also gave some to her husband, who was with her, and he ate it."[18] In that moment, "the eyes of both of them were opened"[19] and all of humanity was doomed.

God, while walking in his garden, discovered the iniquity of Adam and the woman. He called to Adam and asked, "Have you eaten from the tree that I commanded you not to eat from?"[20] But instead of taking responsibility for his own actions, Adam shifted the blame to both God and the woman. "The woman you put here with me—she gave me some fruit from the tree, and I ate it."[21] It is only when she has been accused of breaking His commandment that God speaks to the woman. When asked what she had done, the woman answered simply that "the serpent deceived me, and I ate."[22]

God's punishment was swift and severe. For his role in the fall of man, the serpent was cursed to crawl on his belly and eat dust for the entirety of his life. God also saw fit to ensure that the serpent and woman would never conspire together again, and permanently set them as enemies. Man, he decided, would be forced to toil and work the ground as his punishment. Sustenance would no longer be guaranteed. Adam, and all men, would have to work to survive until they were returned to the earth from which they were taken.

Reserving his greatest punishment for the woman, God declared, "I will make your pains in childbearing very severe; with painful labor you will give birth to children. Your desire will be for your husband, and he will rule over you."[23] Never again would a woman desire knowledge. Never again would a woman rebel. She would be a servant to her husband and no more. Only then, after their fates had been decided, did Adam name his wife Eve, "because she would become the mother of all the living."[24]

Fearing that Adam and Eve might be tempted to eat from the other forbidden tree in the Garden, the Tree of Life whose fruits granted immortality, God banished them from Paradise. To ensure that they could never return, "he placed on the east side of the Garden of Eden cherubim and a flaming sword flashing back and forth to guard the way to the Tree of Life."[25] The fall of humanity was complete.

Like all creation myths, the story of Genesis reflected the attitudes and agendas of the people that composed it. Throughout the ancient world, the great Mother Goddess in all her various incarnations, had been responsible for the gift of life. The details may have changed from people to people, but her sacred role as the progenitor of life was almost universal. And that was a threat to the One God of the Hebrews. Delve a bit deeper and Genesis becomes a profound story of the death of the Mother Goddess.

When the Hebrew God ascended the throne of heaven, a distinct shift began to take place. No longer did life come from the womb of the divine feminine. God needed no balancing female energy. He simply willed life into existence. The sacred role of conception would afterward be given solely to man.

Women were simply incubators, sentenced by God to suffer in child birth but to have no other role in the formation of life. The goddess had been stripped of her most basic and ancient role.

Usurping the role of creator was not enough for God. Under the goddess, death had not been absolute. It was simply a momentary transition in the never-ending cycle of life linking birth to rebirth. Death only became a finality after sin entered the world through Adam and Eve. In his punishment to man, God had declared, "For dust you are, and to dust you will return."[26] Death became a void, a destination rather than a state of renewal. Life began and ended with the Hebrew God.

Throughout Genesis, the Biblical writers masterfully corrupted ancient symbols of the goddess in an effort to further illustrate the superiority of their God. At the heart of man's downfall had stood two great and magnificent trees – trees the goddess Asherah might have someday been worshiped under. Representing life and wisdom, domains of the goddess, the trees were forbidden by the God that had planted them. Man could not touch them or eat of their fruit without facing the finality of the grave. The connotation was clear. To worship the goddess, to even acknowledge her existence, led to death.

One of the oldest religious motifs in the world, the serpent was also corrupted by the story of Genesis. Once a revered symbol of both god and goddess, the serpent could be found throughout the ancient world from Egypt to Mesoamerica to China. Our ancestors had recognized the regenerative power of the snake as it shed its skin, emerging as if reborn again and again. It became a symbol of wisdom, strength, and renewal. Serpent worship was already well established in Canaan long before the arrival of the first Israelites. Many artifacts, including those that depict Lilith, portray powerful goddesses in the presence of snakes. The authors of Genesis, rather craftily, transformed one of the most sacred symbols of antiquity into the greatest villain of the Old Testament. This perversion of the serpent proved to be one of the most successful campaigns against polytheism ever launched by the Hebrews.

After the fourth chapter of Genesis, Eve does not appear again in the Bible. No history of her life or death was written down. When her son Cain murdered his brother Abel, no record was made of her mourning. The names of her daughters have been lost. The "mother of all living" faded into shadow, forgotten like the mother goddesses of old. But the repercussions of her choice in the Garden of Eden lived on in every woman that came after her.

In the Old Testament book of Ezekiel it is stated, "The son shall not bear the iniquities of the father, neither shall the father bear the iniquity of the son."[27] But this separation of guilt did not apply to Eve or the rest of womankind. The words of early Christian theologian Tertullian, sometimes called the founder of Western theology, reflected the general consensus on women: "Do you not believe that you are an Eve? The sentence of God on this sex of yours lives on even in our times, and so it is necessary that guilt should live on, also."[28] The iniquity of Eve became the justification for the repression of women across the Judeo-Christian world.

Throughout the Bible, and other influential texts, the malevolence of women was cited as the basis for their subjugation. Because Eve desired wisdom, all women were condemned forever. There could be no penance great enough to wash away the sins of the mother of all. In a letter outlining proper worship practices, the apostle Paul stated, "A woman should learn in quietness and full submission. I do not permit a woman to teach or to assume authority over a man; she must be quiet. For Adam was formed first, then Eve. And Adam was not the one deceived; it was the woman who was deceived and became a sinner." [29]

During the Burning Times of the 16th century, Eve's downfall was often cited as a justification for the atrocities committed against women accused of witchcraft. A church report justifying the torture of "witches" read, "There was a defect in the formation of the first woman, since she was formed with a bent rib. She is imperfect and thus always deceives."[30] These ideals of the nefarious and cunning nature of women became so ingrained into religion and society as a whole that women throughout the world still struggle to prove their equality and worth to their male counterparts.

Eve's story may have ended with Genesis, but Lilith's was far from over. According to the Talmud, a collection of writings on Jewish law and traditions, when Adam saw that death had entered the world through his and Eve's sin, he separated himself from Eve for a period of 130 years. During that time, Adam was said to have produced ghostly and demonic children with an evil succubus that took advantage of his uncontrollable nightly emissions. And although the Talmud doesn't name Adam's consort, over time the connection became clear. It was the evil Lilith, scorned and angry, that returned to Adam during his sojourn.

From her home on the banks of the Red Sea, Lilith had witnessed the expulsion of Adam and Eve from Eden. She knew of their sin, but as she had left the Garden before the Fall, was not subject to the punishment inflicted upon them. Although she loathed Adam for his domineering attitude, she still desired him greatly. While Adam fasted, separated from Eve, Lilith took advantage of the opportunity before her. From their unholy union, Adam became not only the father of humans but the plagues of humankind as well. As a result, men were warned to never sleep in a house alone. Whoever did so would be "seized by Lilith"[31] and his seed used to unleash new evils into the world.

Men were not the only ones that needed to fear Lilith. Indeed, her greatest enemy was woman. Robbed of her chance to birth mortal children, the early Jews believed Lilith preyed heavily on pregnant women. From barrenness to miscarriage to death of mother or child, complications in childbirth were often seen as Lilith's handiwork. To protect against her wrath, amulets were placed around the home of the pregnant woman and a ring of coal surrounded the birthing room. Inscriptions such as "Adam and Eve. Out Lilith!" were common throughout the ancient Jewish world.[32] Similar amulets were still in use as late as the 20th century as Lilith continued to stalk the lives of the faithful.

Lilith's relationship with newborn children, however, was more complicated. Having declared her purpose as child-killer to the angels, it was accepted that the sudden death of a baby was the work of Lilith. Surprisingly, other much more tender interactions were attributed to her as well. When a baby was seen smiling in its sleep, particularly on the eve of the Sabbath or during a new moon, Lilith was said to be playing with the child.[33] Parents were instructed to tap the infant on the nose three times to expel Lilith's influence. The knot often found in the hair of babies was also attributed to Lilith as her tickling caused the baby to move about and tangled the hair. These sweet, and seemingly innocent, interactions were very uncharacteristic of the villainous Lilith. Perhaps, in those gentle moments, her rage was temporarily forgotten. At least until she was once again cast out by a frantic mother, fearing for the life of her newborn child.

Although the details in the Talmud are scant, a wealth of information was discovered in Nippur, an ancient Mesopotamian city located in modern day Iraq. During excavations of the site, archaeologists from the University of Pennsylvania discovered a large cache of clay tablets, bowls, and inscriptions. More than half of the bowls uncovered contained references to Lilith. Engraved into the bowls were magical incantations against the fury of the she-demon. One such inscription read in part, "The evil Lilith, who causes the hearts of men to go astray and appears in the dream of the night and in the vision of the day, who burns and casts down with nightmare, attacks and kills children, boys and girls." Similar bowls have been found throughout the ancient world from Babylonia to Persia. As these bowls represented the beliefs of the common people and not the religious elite, they provided an important portrait of her reign of terror among early Jewish communities. [34]

In the 13th century, a Spanish writer named Moses de Leon compiled a collection of midrashic commentary into the Zohar, or Book of Splendor, and added a unique new chapter to the already ancient story of Lilith. Heavily mystical in its teachings, the Zohar focuses on the nature of God and attempts to unravel the mysteries of the universe and spirit. It is undoubtedly the most important work of Jewish mysticism, also known as Kabbalah, and contains 56 passages that name or allude to Lilith.

For those not versed in the language of Kabbalah, reading the Zohar can prove a daunting task. That difficulty is further enhanced by the multiple, contradictory tales that it includes. Multiple accounts of the birth of Lilith are given in the Zohar and other important Kabbalistic texts, many of them strikingly different from the previous tales of the Talmud and *The Alphabet*. Other stories tell of Lilith's marriage to Samael (Satan) and emphasize her recurrent role as succubus and child-killers. While these tales are beyond the scope of this book, they are fascinating reading for anyone interested in learning more of the complex saga of Lilith.

Lilith's story may have taken many paths, but they all followed the same pattern. She began as a lowly demon, preying on men, harming women, and killing children. But over time, as with all ancient goddesses, she evolved. In Sumer, she became a goddess of terrible power. In Kabbalah, she eventually became the consort of God himself (more on that in the next chapter). Lilith could not be contained. Not by Adam or angel or God. And not by time. The heart of Lilith endured, virtually unchanged, for four thousand years.

When the early fathers of the Judeo-Christian faith set out to destroy the goddess worship of antiquity, they did so in many ways. When possible, they ripped down her altars and defiled her sacred sites. But when that proved ineffective, they stripped her of her symbols and the domain of her powers. God may have supplanted her place in the cosmos, but her memory would prove a far more formidable foe.

Within the Bible, the goddess is often hidden in plain sight. She is shrouded in darkness, her imagery distorted by those that wished to depose her, but her spirit endures. By definition, perhaps Lilith and Eve do not qualify as true goddesses. They were not deities in their own right as Asherah had been. No shrines were ever erected in their honor. Their names were never called out in prayer. But together, they represented the dual nature of the very Mother Goddess that the Hebrews had worked so hard to destroy. Lilith was the avenging mother, brutal and unforgiving as a raging cyclone. Eve was the doting mother, gentle and loving as a cool summer breeze. One gave life, and the other took life away. Together they embodied the Divine Feminine and ensured that the sacred spark of the goddess survived.

In recent years, as feminism has grown into a worldwide phenomenon, women have begun to reclaim the power stolen from their foremothers. No longer willing to retreat into the shadows, women have embraced Lilith's desire for independence, equality, and sexual freedom. Her name has become a rallying cry for those wishing to separate themselves from outdated patriarchal attitudes. Long shunned for being weak and subservient, Eve is now praised for her desire for knowledge and for the bravery it took to reach for it. At long last, the wives of Adam have taken their rightful place as the mothers of womanhood.

Chapter Four

The Glory

The Hebrews watched in awe as a great cloud descended from heaven and settled within the Temple, filling it with a radiance too brilliant to truly behold. Before them spread the Glory of God, the pillar of cloud and fire that had led them from their bondage in Egypt, the Holy Spirit made manifest. They fell to their knees in thanks and praise. At last, the Shekinah was home.

Asherah had been buried. Lilith had been declared the mother of all evils, and Eve had damned all of humanity to death and peril. The Divine Feminine had been battered and all but forgotten among the children of Yahweh. The goddess had no place in the heaven crafted by the Hebrews, nor in the earth built by the will of their god. Yahweh demanded unwavering allegiance. Any transgressions against that commandment often resulted in brutal showcases of his complete and unforgiving power. This new god had become something wholly unknown in the ancient world – unattainable, lofty, unknowable.

The old gods had undoubtedly been powerful, bending the will of the earth and man with ease. But they had also retained something that Yahweh lacked – a spark of humanity. They had needs and desires, made mistakes, walked among mortals, ate, drank, fought, evolved, and learned. In any situation, a man or woman could look to the ancient heavens and discover common ground with one of the many deities. It made the old gods accessible and bridged the impossible distance between mortal and deity. And it was a dangerous mark of the pagan world that the Hebrews could not tolerate.

Since Biblical times, a major tenet of Judaism has been the total ban of any references or representations of an anthropomorphic

Yahweh.[1] He is simply beyond description. No representation of God is possible as he surpasses the limits of the human imagination. There is no humanity left in the Hebrew God. Religion was no longer based on the personal experience of the sacred. Instead, the Judeo-Christian world would be built on faith alone.

But almost from the beginning, the early fathers of the Church faced a host of problems with their indescribable god. Within their own sacred texts, from the Bible to foundational midrashic literature, they encountered countless references to a man-like Yahweh. In Genesis, He walked among his creations in the Garden of Eden. In Exodus, the covenant was inscribed by the finger of Yahweh himself. Isaiah reported him as sitting on a throne, and in Psalms he was said to dwell in the city of Jerusalem. In fact, it is difficult to find any reference to God (especially in the older texts) where he does not possess some man-like need or ability.

The early Judaic scholars were not blind to this discrepancy in rule and practice. They understood that it could cause confusion among the faithful laypersons. It became their mission to understand and explain these passages in a way that emphasized the transcendent nature of Yahweh while remaining easily grasped by the common Israelite.[2] But by stripping Yahweh of his humanity they bestowed it on the one thing they had so diligently worked to subjugate – the goddess.

Before facing the issues of anthropomorphism in the Torah, a concept had already began to develop within the Jewish communities that would greatly affect the way the early fathers approached reconciling the problematic verses. This idea led to a belief in intermediaries, semi-divine beings that interacted with humanity on God's behalf.[3] This development resulted in a glimpse of the revived goddess in Judaism. An unnamed Wisdom Goddess, an amalgamation of Asherah and other ancient goddesses, began to take shape as one of these intermediaries.

And to truly understand the Shekinah, a brief look at Wisdom is necessary.

Although she is mentioned throughout the Bible, the Book of Proverbs provides a wealth of information on the unnamed entity. In the eighth chapter, Wisdom proclaims herself as the first of God's creations: "When there were no watery depths, I was given birth, when there were no springs overflowing with water; before the mountains were settled in place, before the hills, I was given birth, before he made the world or its fields or any of the dust of the earth."[4] According to this chapter, often referred to as the Call of Wisdom, the goddess is portrayed as having been present during the entire creation of earth and humankind. Other authors will take this idea further and insist that it was Wisdom herself that sparked creation or was perhaps the medium through which God crafted the heavens and earth.[5] Regardless, it is obvious that Wisdom was seen as being an integral part in the mechanism of creation, hearkening back to a time when all was created by the Goddess.

Eventually, Wisdom would take the place of Asherah as the bride of God.[6] No longer would Yahweh's consort be the powerful and overtly sexual goddess of Canaan, but a refined and humble being of knowledge focused solely on the teaching of God and righteousness. But just like the Mother Goddesses of old, Wisdom had another side to her as well. In the first chapter of Proverbs, we find her in an interesting situation usually equated to harlots and prostitutes – crying out in the streets and public square. She rebukes the children of Israel as they ignore her call, promising them "I in turn will laugh when calamity overtakes you"[7] and that "they will eat the fruit of their ways and be filled with the fruit of their schemes."[8]

Wisdom would go on to find even greater importance among the Gnostics, who stressed the importance of knowledge for the salvation of the soul. Under the Gnostic teachings, she would be given a name at long last, Sophia, and became equated with the human soul and the feminine aspect of the Holy Trinity. And while the Gnostic Sophia is beyond the scope of this book, it provides a fascinating subject for anyone interested in learning more about the development of Wisdom.[9]

Although the foundations were laid for Wisdom to become a preeminent goddess figure within Judaism, it simply never happened. Her power waxed and waned, despite the plethora of material written about her in the Bible and the Apocrypha. As with other, older, goddesses, Wisdom evolved and in time was reborn in the powerful Shekinah.

Originating from the Hebrew root *shakhan*, meaning 'to dwell', the name Shekinah originated in the *Onkelos Targum*, an Aramaic translation of the Torah from the 1st-2nd century CE.[10] Like other educated Jewish men, the unknown author of the *Onkelos* wanted to separate Yahweh from the multitude of anthropomorphic references made about him in the Torah. To do this, he introduced the Shekinah, a separate entity from Yahweh, yet one that retained the power of God. Evidence of this is found throughout the *Onkelos* where verses have been altered to reflect this new concept.

The traditional reading of Exodus 25:8, for example, is "then have them make a sanctuary for me, and I will dwell among them." That same passage in the *Onkelos* was rewritten to read, "have them make a sanctuary, and I shall send my Shekinah to dwell among them." Again and again, the Shekinah is invoked in verses as a manifestation of Yahweh. However, at this point in her development, she is merely an aspect of the greater God. Her purpose was only to serve as a personified, visible entity that the faithful could experience in a tangible way. She is a hypostasis, an intermediary, like Wisdom before her.

Within the *Onkelos*, no gender is ever specifically assigned to the concept of the Shekinah. But just as the name of God, Yahweh, stressed his maleness, the name Shekinah grammatically implied a feminine presence. The added *-ah* suffix to the Hebrew *shakhan* made the Shekinah, undeniably, female.[11] No special teachings were needed to implant the idea into the minds of the Hebrews that the Shekinah was a feminine aspect of the Almighty God. Every time her name was repeated, her femininity was confirmed.

Usage of the Shekinah spread quickly and was picked up by other scholars and added to a multitude of *Targums*, of which the *Onkelos* was only one. The influence of the Shekinah grew beyond being solely the aspect of God sent to dwell among the people. She began to be equated to the "glory of God," and even to the "word of God" which had a special connection to the earlier Wisdom Goddess of Proverbs.[12] The Shekinah became the face and hand of God, moving among the people in a way that Yahweh never could. And the Hebrew people began to see her everywhere.

In the earliest days of Judaism, after the Covenant had been struck between Moses and Yahweh, the people had believed that God inhabited the space between the angels that adorned the top of the Ark built to house the sacred tablets inscribed with the Ten Commandments. The Bible states explicitly, "There, above the cover between the two cherubim that are over the ark of the covenant law, I will meet with you and give you all my commands for the Israelites."[13] But how could an incorporeal deity be seen and heard? Indeed, how could he inscribe the law into stone? Simply put, he couldn't. But the Shekinah *could*.

It was not God, the *Targums* insisted, but the Shekinah that appeared between the two golden angels. It was the Shekinah that had appeared as a cloud on Mt. Sinai and spoke to Moses. It was by her hand that the stone tablets of the Covenant were written. She had been the pillar of cloud by day and the pillar of fire by night that had led the Israelites through the wilderness.[14] The Shekinah had fed them, guided them, and taught them. Though she acted on the behalf of God, she did so independently of Him.

The Shekinah was evolving and her influence and power

growing. When Solomon began work on the great Temple of Jerusalem, the Bible records that Yahweh told him, "I will live among the Israelites and will not abandon my people Israel."[15] The *Targums* would change this to reflect the Shekinah and would proclaim the Temple had been built solely for her to dwell within. Until this point, the Shekinah had remained in the Tabernacle or Tents of Meeting that housed the Holy Ark of the Covenant.[16] David, Solomon's father, had erected one of these Tents to house the Ark. (Interestingly enough, after doing so, the pious King David went to Gibeon and praised his God in the holy high place associated with none other than Asherah.)

Upon completion of the Temple, the Ark was brought out of the Tent and placed in the most holy place, the sacred inner altar. Just as the Babylonians and Egyptians before them, the Hebrews believed that their God would physically reside in the Holy of Holies. But it was not Yahweh that took up residence in the Temple. Instead, it was the Shekinah. Once again, she descended in a cloud and "filled the temple of the Lord. And the priests could not perform their service because of the cloud for the glory of the Lord (the Shekinah) filled his temple."[17] The *Onkelos* afterwards refers to the Temple as the "house of the Shekinah." And Rabbi Azaria, writing in the name of the 4th century Palestinian Amora declared that not only did she fill the Temple with her presence but also with her ceaseless love for the Hebrew people.[18]

Of course, as with all religious concepts, disagreements were natural among the men shaping the Judeo-Christian faiths. Some believed that the Shekinah had descended to earth only at the dedication of the Tabernacle, while others believed that she had dwelt on earth since the first moments of creation (possibly even acting as Wisdom with a role in the actual creative process). However, many that believed the Shekinah had always dwelt on earth believed that a series of transgressions by man had caused her to go into exile. The iniquities of her people, from the first moments in Eden to the destruction of the infamous

Sodomites, had caused her to flee and abandon her post among the Hebrews. With each corrupt generation, she had retreated deeper into heaven. It took the actions of seven righteous men – Abraham, Isaac, Jacob, Levi, Kehat, Amram, and Moses – to bring her slowly back to earth and finally into the Ark within the Tabernacle.[19]

With the fall of Jerusalem to Nebuchadnezzar II in 587 BCE, the Israelites found themselves, once again, in exile. The Temple of Solomon was destroyed and the people forced into Babylonia. According to the prophet Ezekiel, the Shekinah had departed the Temple just before the destruction occurred, taking temporary refuge on the Mount of Olives. But just like any mother, her dedication to the Hebrews called to her and she eventually joined them in their diaspora. In the Babylonian city of Nehardea, she found a new home in a synagogue built from the dust of Jerusalem. There she appeared physically to the faithful gathered in study of the Torah. It is from these appearances that we learn that the Shekinah often appeared as a glorious light and to the sound of tinkling bells.[20] For the early Jews it was obvious – wherever they roamed, the Shekinah went with them.

When the Jews were finally allowed back into Judah, and the modest Second Temple constructed, the Shekinah was expected to return to her former seat. Whether she did or not, however, was a subject of great disagreement. Some argued that she remained in the Second Temple continuously, while others believed she only visited the Temple at certain times. Still others maintained that she never dwelt within the new temple at all. The Shekinah's absence, they argued, was one of the many reasons that the second incarnation of the holy dwelling was inferior to the first built by Solomon. The Glory of the God had left, unrestrained by the Temple walls, and had dispersed among the people.[21]

Within the midrashic literature, it is clear that the Shekinah physically manifested among the Hebrews. She sought out those gathered to study the Torah, but she did not limit herself to the educated men of Israel. She also ministered to the spirit of the sick and downtrodden, bringing them comfort in their times of need. Where people gathered to dance and sing in celebration, she manifested among them in their joy. When a sinner took to his knees to ask for forgiveness, the Shekinah wept beside him.

It was not only the faithful that attracted the benefaction of the Shekinah. Even the pagans and idolaters that the Hebrews were so quick to damn were no strangers to the Shekinah.[22] When they gathered in the name of love and hospitality, no matter which deity they called upon, the Shekinah descended and walked among them. It was not simply the act of religious devotion that called to the Shekinah. Kindness and need called to her, and her affection was not limited to or by Yahweh. Her separation from God was complete. She had stepped beyond the Glory of God and into her own divinity.

The earliest evidence of the Shekinah taking her place as a separate entity dates from the 3rd century CE. By this time, the Shekinah had already evolved from the Glory of God to become the Holy Spirit itself. Therefore, from this period on, any reference to the Holy Spirit became a reference to the Shekinah as well. When Rabbi Aha around 300 CE wrote that the Holy Spirit defended Israel before God himself, it was the Shekinah that had actually stood before Yahweh. After admonishing Israel for its sinfulness, she turned to God and said, "Say not: I will do to him as he hath done to me." [23]

By confronting God, the Shekinah displayed the breadth of her own growing prowess. She was a goddess, built from the dust of the vanquished Asherah and molded by the hands of Wisdom. And this did not sit well with some in the Jewish community. Just as her predecessors had been dangerous affronts to the God of the Hebrews, many saw the growing influence of the Shekinah as equally blasphemous. Rabbis warned the faithful to remember that the Shekinah was no more than a physical manifestation of the true God. But by becoming the knowable face of the deity that could not be ascertained or imagined, the Shekinah filled a vacant role left behind by the departure of the Divine Feminine in Judaism.

Like Lilith and Wisdom, the story of the Shekinah developed in even greater detail within the mystical teachings of the Kabbalah. Emerging as the Matronit, the Shekinah became arguably the most important member of the Kabbalistic tetrad. Just as the Shekinah had once interceded between Israel and God, the Matronit was the intermediary between heaven and earth. And she was undeniably heralded as a goddess.[24]

In the same way the Shekinah had remained on earth with her people after the destruction of the Temple, the Matronit tended to Israel when God (or the King in Kabbalah) had retreated to the highest levels of Heaven. This separation diminished the King, however, as without the Matronit he was no longer whole. And this is where Lilith makes her entrance into the story of the Shekinah.

As the Matronit suffered the Babylonian exile with the Hebrews, the King found himself growing bored and lonely. The Matronit had barely stepped foot into Babylonia when the King found himself a new bride to fill the emptiness. From the Matronit's own handmaidens, he choose her replacement – Lilith. Once a lowly she-demon, Lilith reigned as the bride of God.

While the King enjoyed his time with the sultry Lilith, the Matronit found herself at the mercy of foreign gods. The Matronit became unwillingly bound to the children of pagan lands. And just as the Shekinah had walked among the idolaters, so too did the Matronit. Yahweh had demanded the destruction of all that did not worship in his name alone. But in the arms of the Shekinah-Matronit, all were welcome.

According to the Kabbalah, the Matronit remains in exile until this very day. On her throne sits Lilith, delighting in the weakening of the King and the suffering of the Hebrews. Only with the coming of the Messiah will the Matronit be reunited with the King and Lilith destroyed. It is a day that the Jews still await.[25]

Like many of the powerful goddesses before her – Asherah, Inanna, Athena, and countless others – the Shekinah's wise and compassionate aspects were balanced by her terrible ruthlessness in battle. Just as any loving mother, transgressions against her children unleashed a dreadful and deadly side of the goddess. To the Shekinah-Matronit, the King entrusted all of the legions of Heavenly warriors and the entirety of His armaments. Standing ready with the fiery chariots of God, the Shekinah-Matronit waged war against foes both human and divine, delivering holy justice to all who awakened her wrath.[26]

Building on this image of the punitive goddess, the Kabbalah gave the Shekinah yet another role. When the Angel of Death could not touch a particularly righteous man or woman, the Shekinah stepped in to release his or her soul to Heaven. The Talmud records six such individuals – Abraham, Isaac, Jacob, Moses, Aaron, and Miriam. Each was believed to have left this life, not through the reaping of Death, but through a kiss of the Shekinah. [27]

Just as in the Old Testament, the name Shekinah never appears in the New Testament books of the Bible. But this has not stopped many from finding her presence within the story of the Christian messiah, Jesus Christ. Just as in the rabbinical writings, the Shekinah can be interchanged with any New Testament passage discussing the glory of God. When Luke wrote that the shepherds keeping watch over their flocks by night were terrified by the "glory of the Lord"[28] shining about them, the ancient Hebrews would have readily accepted that it was the Shekinah that appeared to herald the coming of Christ. For wherever the light of God shone, the Shekinah was present.

The book of John contains another passage that easily

connected the goddess to the Son of God. John 2:14 states: "The Word became flesh and made his dwelling among us. We have seen his glory, the glory of the one and only Son, who came from the Father, full of grace and truth." Jesus was, the Gospels proclaim, the true Temple of God. Not one built from stone and mortar but raised from blood and bone. The Glory of God, the Shekinah, rested upon him and filled him. Indeed, her influence could even be seen as he prayed. Luke 9:29 proclaimed that as Jesus prayed his face transformed and "his clothes became as bright as a flash of lightning." In the same book, a cloud descended and covered Christ and his disciples and spoke to them, proclaiming Jesus as the Son of God. The cloud was none other than the Shekinah reprising one of her oldest manifestations.

The concept of Christ's glory is mentioned some eighteen times throughout the Gospels, and all can be read in relation to the Shekinah. Paul takes the connection even further when he refers to Jesus as "the Lord of glory,"[29] the same title used nine times in the apocryphal Book of Enoch. While the ancient Hebrews gathered around Moses had been unable to look upon the glorious Shekinah, the followers of Christ were allowed to behold the glory of God through him. References to the glory of Christ can be found throughout the entirety of the New Testament.

It is, of course, quite controversial to link the savior of Christ to a powerful goddess figure. In fact, it could be considered outright blasphemy. But for those writing the chronicles of Jesus, the figure of the Shekinah would have been both familiar and welcomed. So ingrained in to the Jewish mindset was the Shekinah, that she can still be found in modern Judaism. Eventually, the Shekinah evolved into another Jewish representation of the Divine Feminine, the Shabbat Hamalka.[30] Also known as the "Queen of the Sabbath," she is the personification of the Sabbath day of rest. To this day, songs are sung to her every Friday afternoon while women light candles in her honor.

The Shekinah filled a very real need in the heart of Judaism. The comforting presence of the Mother Goddess had been forcibly removed, leaving the people at the mercy of a merciless Father God. The Hebrew people had sworn an oath to Yahweh to serve no other god but him, but still they felt the emptiness left from the departure of the goddess. It is no wonder that, eventually, they found a way to incorporate the feminine back into their faith in a way that did not contradict the belief in One God. The Shekinah is a truly Jewish goddess, built on the remains of the goddesses of old yet unique in her own right. And she would leave her mark on the goddess yet to come.

Today, the Shekinah is embraced by those looking to restore the feminine to faiths built on the masculine. But sadly, she is often overlooked and her power greatly diminished. For the ancient Hebrews, however, she was a being of immense importance. No other aspect of God was more approachable, more comforting, more tangible than the Shekinah. When God abandoned his people, the Shekinah remained. Whether they found themselves in the depths of Egypt, Babylon, or Rome, they knew that the Shekinah walked among them. And as the Jews spread throughout the world, so too did the Shekinah, embracing Jew and Gentile alike. While ruthless when angered, the Shekinah emanated divine love and acceptance. She was, and is, the true Mother Goddess of Judaism.

Chapter Five

The Mother

She felt the world shifting beneath her feet, changing and evolving.
A new world was being born around her, and she stood motionless
in the middle of it all. A child, a mother, a bride to an unknowable
God. And in her heart, Mary pondered the revelations revealed to
her.

Readily welcomed into the Jewish synagogues, the Shekinah found herself evicted from the churches of early Christianity. Although she remained behind the veil of the Holy Spirit, the Shekinah had no place in the newly developing faith. The role of the Divine Feminine stood uninhabited once again, a churning maelstrom among the people so accustomed to a Great Mother's embrace.

The story of the Hidden Goddess continues in the small village of Nazareth in the mountainous region of Galilee. There, a young maiden named Mary lived a quiet and unremarkable life. As a girl of perhaps 14, she probably spent much of her time focused on the domestic needs of her family. It is believed she was a wonderful weaver of tapestries, so perhaps she was busy at her loom when the angel of the Lord appeared to her. It must have been a frightful experience to look up and behold the mighty archangel Gabriel standing before her, his Heavenly voice proclaiming: "Greetings, you who are highly favored! The Lord is with you."[1]

Mary, unsettled by the angel's greeting, pondered the significance of his appearance. Even at such a young age, she understood that what was transpiring was something extraordinary. Seeing her trepidation, the angel said, "Do not be afraid, Mary; you have found favor with God. You will conceive and give birth to a son, and you are to call him Jesus. He will be great and will be called the Son of the Most High."[2]

Undoubtedly, the angel's words gave her little comfort. Mary was a maiden, betrothed to the carpenter Joseph. Admittedly, under Jewish law, Mary and Joseph were already married in all but name. But as Joseph had not yet taken Mary to his own home, the marriage had not been consummated. Confused by the angel's revelation Mary asked, "How will this be since I am a virgin?"[3] Gabriel explained to the bewildered maiden that she would be overshadowed by the Holy Spirit so that her son would be called the Son of God. Mary listened to all that the angel proclaimed and answered, "I am the Lord's servant. May your word to me be fulfilled."[4] With those simple words of acceptance, the story of Christianity began.

Before departing, the angel Gabriel offered Mary a sign of his fidelity. In the hill country of Judah, Elizabeth, Mary's cousin, was pregnant after a lifetime of barrenness with a child of great importance. Mary hurriedly made the journey to the home of Elizabeth and Zechariah and found her cousin was indeed six months pregnant with a child that would become John the Baptist. When she saw Mary, the Holy Spirit filled Elizabeth and the child within her womb leaped with joy. She cried in a loud voice, "Blessed are you among women, and blessed is the child you will bear."[5]

Upon Mary's return to Nazareth, Joseph discovered that she was quite obviously with child. Being a pious and lawful man, Joseph was deeply disturbed by the situation he suddenly found himself in. Pregnancy out of wedlock was no trivial matter at the time. He could have easily cast her away, or even had her killed, for her indiscretion. But, interestingly, he did not wish to expose Mary's disgrace. Many Jewish men might have publicly humiliated her as a sinful woman, but Joseph hesitated and carefully contemplated how he should proceed.

Appearing in a dream, an angel visited Joseph and declared that he not be afraid to take Mary as his wife "because what is conceived in her is from the Holy Spirit."[6] When Joseph awoke, he went to Mary and brought her home as his wife. However, Matthew is quick to record that the marriage was not consummated until after the birth of the child.[7]

When Caesar Augustus ordered a census of the entire Roman world, Joseph took the heavily pregnant Mary with him to Bethlehem to be registered. While there, Mary felt the first pains of labor. Finding no room for them at the inn, Mary gave birth and placed her son in a manger.

Nearby, an angel appeared to a group of shepherds and announced the birth of Jesus: "Today in the town of David a Savior has been born to you; he is the Messiah, the Lord. This will be a sign to you – you will find a baby wrapped in cloths and lying in a manger."[8] The shepherds hurriedly sought the child and, upon finding Mary and Joseph, went among the people declaring all that they had experienced. They returned again to the manger and glorified and praised God for all they had seen and heard. "But Mary treasured up all these things and pondered them in her heart."[9]

When presenting their son at the temple for consecration, Mary was greeted by Simeon, a righteous man promised by the Holy Spirit that he would not die until he had beheld the Lord's Messiah. Seeing the newborn in Mary's arms, he took the child from her and prayed, "Sovereign Lord, as you have promised, you may now dismiss your servant in peace. For my eyes have seen your salvation, which you have prepared in the sight of all nations; a light for revelation to the Gentiles, and the glory of your people Israel."[10] But Simeon also issued a warning to Mary, one that would seem to justify her initial fears, "This child is destined to cause the falling and rising of many in Israel, and to be a sign that will be spoken against, so that the thoughts of many hearts will be revealed. And a sword will pierce your own soul too."[11] As she always had, Mary kept these revelations close to her heart and reflected on their meaning.

Not long after the birth of Jesus, and the visitation of the three magi from the east, Joseph was once again visited by an angel in his dreams. This time the angel came with a warning to flee from their homeland. Herod, disturbed by rumors of a newborn "King of the Jews," had ordered the slaughter of all baby boys in and around Bethlehem. For three years the Holy Family sought refuge in Egypt until the angel reappeared and told them it was safe to return home. It was only through this divine intervention that Jesus was spared during the Massacre of the Innocents that robbed innumerable families of their sons, a burden that undoubtedly weighed heavily on the heart of the young Mary.

Although the story of the nativity is familiar to most, the rest of Mary's life is mentioned only in brief moments recorded throughout the Gospels. Luke presented her as a worried mother, searching for her son in Jerusalem after realizing he had not returned with them from the Passover Festival. For three days she and Joseph searched for the 12 year old Jesus before finding him within the Temple. It isn't difficult to imagine the relief and frustration she felt at finding her son sitting among the teachers who looked at Jesus in disbelief and amazement. Her emotions bubbled forth, and she cried, "Son, why have you treated us like this? Your father and I have been anxiously searching for you."[12] Jesus, seemingly irritated at her outburst answered, "Why were you searching for me? Didn't you know I had to be in my Father's house?"[13] The curtness of his reply would repeat itself in subsequent appearances of Mary in the New Testament.

Mary next appeared with Jesus and his disciples at a wedding in Cana. Approaching her son, Mary informed him that the wine had ran out and asked him to intercede. Why she felt compelled to act is uncertain, but she clearly believed that her son had the ability to remedy the situation. Jesus, however, was annoyed by her request. He answered her, "Woman, why do you involve me? My hour has not yet come."[14] Despite his irritable and somewhat disrespectful tone, Mary instructed the servants to do whatever Jesus requested, and they gathered around him to await their instructions. Seeing that he had no choice, Jesus directed them to fill six jars with water. When the servants dipped into the jars to draw forth the water, they found that it had been turned into wine. It was at the behest of his mother that Jesus performed his first miracle – a point that would inspire countless beliefs and prayers in the centuries to come.

In two of her final appearances, Mary was again treated less than admirably by her son. While Jesus was teaching in Capernaum, the book of Luke testifies that his mother and brothers journeyed to see him. However, because of the crowd, they were unable to get close to him. Word traveled through the crowd until it reached Jesus who answered shortly, "My mother and brothers are those who hear God's word and put it into practice."[15] Mary must surely have been heartbroken, and whether or not she ever met with her beloved son on that day is unknown.

After the incident in Capernaum, Mary disappeared yet again from the narrative until the time of the Crucifixion. She wept and mourned at the feet of her dying son, the sword piercing her own soul just as Simeon had foretold, suffering in a way only a mother truly can. Seeing her there, Jesus looked down to her and again addressed her simply as "woman" and put her into the care of his disciple John.

After the death of Jesus, Mary is mentioned only one other time in a simple reference about her presence among the apostles in the Book of Acts. When Jesus was resurrected after three days, he did not seek out his mother. Her eyes never beheld the risen savior, her firstborn son. She had been the vessel that brought forth the Son of God and nothing more. She retreated into the shadow of his glory. There is not even a mention of her death, for once her purpose was completed, Mary was of little consequence to the early church.

For many years, Mary's potential remained quietly forgotten. If she was mentioned at all, it was as a mere metaphor for the church itself (just as the Shekinah had first emerged as nothing more than the dwelling place of God).[16] But just as the Shekinah had evolved, Mary would as well. Although she spoke only four times in the Bible, the devoted and mournful mother captured the hearts of the early Christians. Slowly, she began to emerge from the pages of the New Testament, not as only the mother of Christ, but as the chosen one of God.

In an attempt to fill in the missing pieces of Mary's life, countless non-canonical texts began to emerge around the second century. One of the most important of these apocryphal writings was the Gospel of James, written circa 145 CE. Mary's parents are introduced in the text as Joachim and Anne, who like Elizabeth and Zechariah, lamented their inability to conceive a child. Praying fervently, an angel finally appeared and delivered the news that Anne would conceive a child of such great importance that her name would be known throughout the world. In thanks, Joachim and Anne pledge to dedicate their daughter to the service of the temple.[17]

That child was, of course, the Blessed Virgin Mary. A prodigy from an extraordinarily young age, the author of the Book of James records that, in keeping with the vow of her parents, Mary was dedicated to the Temple at the age of three and danced with joy on the altar steps. Angels attended to her and fed her as she wove beautiful veils to adorn the Temple. But fearing that she might defile the sanctity of the Temple through menstruation at puberty, a suitable guardian was sought for her. (Note that it was not necessarily a marriage which the priests arranged for her. This point will be very important in the centuries to come.) After receiving a sign from God, the widowed Joseph was chosen to care for the maiden and took her into his home with his other children.[18]

Drawing on the Book of James and other writings, Mary's

virginity became a point of great discourse in the early Church. While the story of the virgin birth had appeared in the books of Matthew and Luke, written sometime around 70 to 90 CE, the older text of Mark makes no mention of it. John also never cites the supernatural birth of Jesus despite having been written after the traditions of Matthew and Luke were established. The supernal conception of Christ did not begin to gain importance till several decades after his death.

Some factions, such as the Ebionites, outright denied that Jesus had been conceived in any exceptional way and was as much Joseph's son as he was Mary's. But these beliefs were quickly labeled heretical and dismissed. The very bedrock that the Church had been built upon depended on the divinity of Jesus. And in the ancient world, birth from a virgin or through the coupling with a god was an unquestionable sign of holiness and eminence. It was a scenario that had played out in countless cultures already as virgin goddesses gave birth to heroes and disguised gods joined with mortal women. The difference, however, between those accounts and Mary's was important – no god had overpowered or defiled her in the conception of her child. The Christ child had appeared intact, within her womb, with no interaction on her part.

For a people that typically viewed sex as a doorway to sin and death, the early church spent a great deal of time debating the bedroom life of Mary and Joseph. The Book of Matthew, likely written within a generation of the events it recorded, very clearly stated that Joseph and Mary had consummated their marriage after the birth of Jesus.[19] Both Matthew and Mark list James, Joseph, Judas, and Simon as the brothers of Jesus along with at least three anonymous sisters. In this instance, the Bible is unusually clear – Jesus had siblings. But this idea was anathema to the early Christian fathers. The womb that bore the Messiah, they argued, could never carry mere mortal children. And once chosen by the Almighty himself, Mary would have never allowed herself to be defiled by a man, not even her own earthly husband.

Looking back on the Gospel of James, Christians began to weave a new picture of Mary. Not only as the virgin that had birthed the Savior but also as the Ever Virgin who remained untainted by man throughout the entirety of her life.[20] The brothers and sisters of Jesus named in the Old Testament were simply the children of the elderly Joseph and an unnamed first wife. Furthermore, Joseph had never been the husband of Mary despite the references to such in the New Testament. He was simply the caretaker of the Virgin who, as a female, had to be under the guardianship of a man. They were husband and wife in name alone.

Of course, other explanations also sprang forth to clarify the issue of Jesus' siblings. Some believed that they were simply cousins of Jesus, the children of Joseph's sister (who was also named Mary). Having grown up with these cousins, Jesus considered them his brothers and sisters. Still others proclaimed they were no more than close friends with a special relationship to Christ.

Whatever view one took, by the fourth century the belief in the perpetual virginity of Mary was widely supported by the Church. In 649, the Lateran Council affirmed the teachings of Mary's virginity before, during, and after the birth of Jesus.[21] The modern Catholic Church still holds that birthing Christ did not diminish Mary's virginity and that Jesus was the only child ever born to the Blessed Mother.

Growing alongside the doctrine of perpetual virginity, the image of Mary as Second Eve began to also gain momentum.[22] First introduced by the Christian apologist and philosopher Justin Martyr around the mid-second century, Mary emerged as the spiritual and virtuous antithesis of the doomed mother of humanity. The idea was sparked by the writings of the apostle Paul in which he referred to Christ as the new Adam in the books of Romans and 1 Corinthians. Just as Christ had been born to redeem men from the sins of Adam, Mary would do the same for womankind. Through emulating the chaste and demure ways of the Virgin, women could free themselves from Eve's burden. And that meant denouncing sex completely and taking a vow of lifelong chastity.

For many that are familiar with the myths surrounding the Wheel of the Year, an interesting connection to the polytheistic world is evoked when Mary and Jesus are equated to Adam and Eve. Throughout the ancient world, stories existed around the changing of seasons and stressed a divine son/spouse relationship. To summarize a rather fascinating story, the goddess gives birth to the god who then becomes her spouse. The god dies, usually through self-sacrifice, and is then reborn to the goddess. Each step within the drama corresponds to the cycles of the natural world. As Jesus was both God and the Son of God, Mary was both the wife (or at least, the latest wife in a long line of forgotten goddesses) *and* mother of God. Her son willingly went to his death on the cross to save the souls of humanity, just as the ancient god gave his own essence to ensure that life would continue through the harshness of winter.

Not unaware of the similarities between Christ and other savior gods – especially Osiris, Adonis, and Mithras – the early Christians actively discouraged the comparison of Jesus to older deities. Those deities, they argued, were false gods and demons sent to diminish the glory of Jesus Christ even before his physical birth.[23] To discourage the connection of Second Eve to the stories of the goddess, they chose to focus on the redemptive aspect of the Virgin. As humanity had been damned by a female, it was only natural that it be a female that birthed salvation. Though that salvation was meant to be seen as transpiring through Christ, eventually focus began to shift to the Virgin herself. Just as Wisdom and the Shekinah had become mediators between man and God, so too did the Virgin Mary. More easily accessible than her son, Mary began to build a following that considered her a co-redeemer with Christ, someone that would stand before God and argue for the salvation of the sinner that called upon her name.

There were some, however, that did not shy away from the connections of Mary to the goddess. The Collyridians, first referenced by Church Father Epiphanius around 375 in his collection of heresies, were a sect that openly worshiped the Holy Mother as a goddess. Although we know very little about the beginnings of the Collyridians (or even what they called themselves as "collyridians" was a derogatory nickname given to them by Epiphanius), it is evident that they drew their beliefs and practices from the pre-Christian world. And their actions directly tied Mary to Asherah, the first goddess of the Hebrews.[24]

Epiphanius records that by the time of his writing, the Collyridian influence had already spread from its beginnings in Thrace into Arabia and the lands surrounding the Black Sea. Consisting of mostly women, the Collyridians worshiped Mary as the Queen of Heaven, a title borrowed from Asherah. Their rituals lasted for days and included the baking of cakes or bread for the goddess, just as Jeremiah had recorded was done for Asherah centuries earlier. Arguably, the Collyridians represent the first true Marian cult, who in the presence of a harsh god chose Mary to reign as the Mother Goddess.[25]

While Mary's perpetual virginity and the virgin birth of Jesus obviously set her apart from the average woman, it will still not enough for early Christians. To have been worthy of birthing the savior, they argued, Mary must have been special from the moment of her birth. Certainly God must have known that she would bear his son long before she herself was conceived. These thoughts gave rise to the belief in the Immaculate Conception. Mary, alone in the annals of humanity, had been born without the stain of original sin. An idea often touted by the theologian Augustine, original sin was the belief that every human child was born bearing the curse of Adam and Eve. As such, even newborns were subject to the punishments allotted in the Garden of Eden. Yahweh had set Mary apart from every other living soul in preparation for birthing the Son of God.[26]

The belief in Mary's Immaculate Conception, however, led to another problem. The punishment for sin was death. Because of the fall of Adam and Eve, all of humanity was destined to die. But what of Mary, who had been born without original sin? Had she suffered the desecration of death?

The Bible does not record Mary's death in any manner. And just like in other instances when the Biblical text was lacking desired details, apocryphal texts and traditions stepped in to provide the answers. Although the stories varied, eventually they would merge into two complementary beliefs – the dormition and the assumption. Despite very small differences in the two beliefs, both recognize that Mary reached the end of her life, died in some manner, and was assumed body and soul into heaven. Both doctrines are still held in various branches of the Church and further illustrate the unique blessings afforded to the Virgin.[27]

Death was not the end for the Virgin Mary, regardless of how it did or did not transpire. Her life as the Mother of God had barely been touched on within the Bible, but it did little to temper her influence on the development of Christianity. By the fifth century, feasts honoring Mary (by association with the Nativity of Jesus) had already been established within the Church. More feasts, dedicated solely to the Virgin, would emerge by the 7th century. Countless works of art, poems, and liturgies had been produced in her honor. Her image adorned the greatest cathedrals and the humblest of homes. Popes and commoners alike bent their knee to her. Throughout the Christian world, the faithful called upon her in their darkest hours.[28]

And the Virgin answered. The devoted around the world have reported miraculous visitations of the Blessed Mother, often referred to as Marian apparitions, since her death. But the earliest of these reportedly happened while the Virgin was still alive, in the year 40 CE. It was recorded that while the Virgin lived in Jerusalem, she appeared atop a jasper pillar to St. James while he prayed in Zaragoza, Spain. Telling James that his efforts to convert the pagans would not be in vain, she then asked him to build a church in her honor at the site of her appearance. He did as she asked, and the first Marian shrine in history was erected by the Ebro River.

More and more reports of Marian apparitions followed from the Holy Lands to Mexico. Like the Shekinah, wherever her people roamed, the Virgin Mary went with them. Throughout Christendom, she stood ready to answer the pleas of her children. For if all men had been reborn through Jesus Christ, humanity had inherited a new Great Mother.

To her children, the Virgin dispensed knowledge, prophecy, and healing. At times, she even left behind gifts as in the beautiful image of Our Lady of Guadalupe miraculously imprinted into the cloak of Saint Juan Diego. In Lourdes, France she led a young girl to the location of a healing spring where beneficial waters continue to bless the faithful to this day. In Fatima, Portugal, the Virgin divulged secret prophecies to three children (and appeared to them cloaked in light, an image first associated with the Shekinah).[29] Today, Marian devotion is alive and well throughout the Catholic and Orthodox churches. Reverence nearing worship is commonplace. And although the faithful vehemently deny the exaltation of Mary as a goddess within the Church, it exists beneath the trappings of a monotheistic belief as it always has. Mary was fashioned from the goddesses of old – Asherah, Wisdom, the Shekinah – and so many more beyond the Israelite world. Perhaps it is because of this that she has been welcomed into the ranks of the goddess among many modern pagans who recognize her as an incarnation of the Mother Goddess. And, like the Shekinah, she welcomes her pagan children into the same arms that hold the faithful.

While the goddess imagery connected to Mary is not new or unique to Christianity, one thing is: Mary is undeniably human. She was born of human parents, despite any special blessings concerning her conception or purity. She grew and lived as a mortal girl until one interaction with the divine altered the course of her life. Did Mary have an actual choice in bearing the Son of God? Could she have denied the Holy Spirit? Did God rob her of her autonomy? These are questions without answers, but the fact remains that Mary, a simple girl living an ordinary life, became the Mother of God. She was not born divine. She was *made* divine. Not by God, but by the people that devoted their hearts to her.

Chapter Six

The Heiress

The tomb was empty. All that remained were the white cloths that had been draped across his broken body. She stood motionless, tears streaking down her face. The jar of anointing oil rattled quietly in her trembling hands. Where had they taken him? Panic began to fill her heart until a familiar voice rang out through the silence, calling her name – Mary Magdalene.

For all the glories bestowed on her, the Virgin Mary was, in reality, a very minor character in the New Testament narrative. Her purpose was to bear the Son of God and nothing more. Her exaltation by the Church and her followers, however, placed her in a unique position. She was both human and divine, a lofty and impossible standard to which women were to be held. By setting her apart from all others in remarkable and miraculous ways, the Church was able to mold her into the face of the goddess that best suited their own needs.

But as history has shown, the goddess is not easily regulated or diminished. Even today, in a world ruled by the three great monotheistic faiths, she is rising. No longer the demure and accepting Virgin, this incarnation is a fearless rebel, unafraid to question authority and to forge her own path. With the power of Asherah, the curiosity of Eve, the passion of Lilith, the faith of the Shekinah, and the heart of the Virgin, the goddess is being reborn.

Mary Magdalene's story began in Galilee. As Jesus traveled between villages preaching the word of God, Mary Magdalene was among the women that accompanied him. The book of Luke recorded, "The Twelve were with him, and also some women who had been cured of evil spirits and diseases: Mary (called

Magdalene) from whom seven demons had come out; Joanna the wife of Chuza, the manager of Herod's household; Susanna; and many others."[1] Luke then goes on to offer an intriguing bit of information – the women were supporting Jesus' ministry "out of their own means."[2]

Jesus may have been ahead of his time with his acceptance of females within his inner echelon, but the women who traveled with him were absolute revolutionaries. In a time dominated by harsh Jewish laws that diminished womankind to mere property, Mary Magdalene and her friends were living independent lives beyond the reach of fundamental Judaism. They were also, as Luke mentioned, independently wealthy, using their own money to finance Jesus' ministry.

Although we know nothing of the early life of Mary Magdalene, Luke provided enough to piece together some of her history. Mary was a Hellenised Jew, a product of Greek and Roman cultures filtering through the Holy Land. As her money indicated, she was probably a member of an upper-class family able to bend, or even ignore, the rules set out by the Jewish faith.[3] She was educated, inquisitive, and dedicated to the teachings of Jesus.

Mary Magdalene was mentioned by name only fourteen times in the Bible but each appearance is crucial to the Christ story. She was with him as he preached, baptized, and proclaimed that the Kingdom of Heaven was at hand. When he was scourged and drenched in blood and sweat, Mary Magdalene was there. She heard the cries of the people demanding his crucifixion. She, and the other women that had devoted their lives to Jesus, followed him to Golgotha and watched helplessly as he was nailed to the cross. All four gospels agree that she was there to witness the death of the Savior. Whether she watched from a distance or wept at his feet, she was there. And when it was finally finished, and Jesus was dead, she followed as his body was carried away and placed in the tomb provided by Joseph of Arimathea.

The Bible provided only hints at the relationship that Mary Magdalene shared with Jesus. We know that her name was always recorded before the names of other women. That she was accorded a special place in his ministry and life is undoubted. But was there more? Could she have been the wife of the Son of God?

On the third day after the crucifixion, Mary Magdalene set out quietly for the tomb of Jesus. In her hands she carried a jar of precious oils. As was traditional, she went to clean and anoint the body of the crucified Christ. A simple act but one that carried a tremendous implication. Within the tomb, Jesus lay naked, covered only by a thin white cloth. As independent as Mary Magdalene may have been, touching or seeing the nude body of a man that wasn't her husband or close relative would have been absolutely forbidden. Jesus had a living mother, possibly sisters, aunts, or cousins that should have attended to him in death. Instead, it was Mary Magdalene that approached the tomb.

According to the book of John, Mary Magdalene found that the stone covering the entrance to the tomb had been rolled away. She immediately fled, running to Simon Peter and another disciple to tell them of the disturbance. The men ran to the tomb and discovered it was open and empty but did not understand the implications. Instead, they simply returned to the place where they had been staying.[4]

Mary, however, was distraught. She remained behind, alone and weeping. Entering the tomb, Mary was greeted by two angels in white who asked her why she wept. She answered quietly, "They have taken my Lord away, and I don't know where they have put him."[5] As she turned to leave, she discovered a man standing before her. Just as the angels had, the man asked Mary the reason for her tears. Thinking he was the gardener, Mary cried, "Sir, if you have carried him away, tell me where you have put him, and I will get him."[6]

Alone in the tomb, Mary wept in front of the angels. Did she realize they were heavenly messengers? Perhaps her grief was too deep, too raw for her to care in that moment. Her mind was only on the missing body of the one she so deeply loved. So complete was her sorrow that she did not even recognize the man standing in the entrance of the tomb. Until he said simply, "Mary." When Jesus called her name, she knew immediately that it was the risen Christ standing before her, and she instinctively reached out her hand to touch him.[7]

The other gospels recorded the event somewhat differently, placing other women with Mary Magdalene at the tomb. Matthew recorded that an angel rolled the stone away to reveal the empty tomb to the women. Mark wrote that two angels were within the tomb when the women approached. Luke also wrote of angels that appeared to Mary and her companions.[8] In each gospel, the women were the first at the empty tomb and were told to take the news of the Resurrection to the disciples who do not believe until Jesus himself appeared to them. But Mary Magdalene's faith never wavered and she was rewarded by witnessing the risen Christ, a blessing not even afforded to his own mother.

As Michael Haag wrote in *The Quest for Mary Magdalene*, "Mary Magdalene is the only person close to Jesus at the critical moments that define his purpose, that describe his fate, and that will give rise to a new religion."[9] Her faith in him was absolute. But once Jesus was dead and resurrected, Mary Magdalene disappeared from the Biblical narrative. Her name was not mentioned in the Acts of the Apostles or in the many books written by or about Paul. She simply vanished, leaving the rest of her story to the imagination.

Or did she?

Just as it had happened so many times before, stories of Mary developed throughout the ancient world. Perhaps among the most famous and remarkable was the belief that Mary and others escaped Palestine in a boat with no oars. The boat was then miraculously transported to the south of France where

Mary and her companions worked to convert the pagans of the country. When their conversion was complete, Mary retreated into the wilderness in penance for her sins. But what sins had the beloved of Jesus committed?

Unfortunately for Mary Magdalene, her introduction in Luke came directly after an incident that occurred in the early days of Jesus' ministry. Luke recorded that while dining at the house of Simon the Pharisee, a sinful woman entered and knelt before Jesus. Using her tears, she washed his feet and dried them with her hair. She then anointed him with precious and costly ointments while Jesus' host looked on in horror. Appalled, Simon asked Jesus why he would allow such a sinful woman to touch him. After admonishing Simon for failing to wash his feet or anoint him with oil, Jesus declared, "Therefore, I tell you, her many sins have been forgiven—as her great love has shown."[10]

Luke did not record the nature of the woman's iniquities. But for the early Church, her sins were as obvious as her sex. As though it were the worst evil a woman could possibly commit, she was branded a whore. And although there is no mention of the woman's name, history (and a sixth century pope named Gregory the Great) would assign her sins to Mary Magdalene. By the time her story reached France, Mary Magdalene's role as the penitent whore was complete. The connection between Mary Magdalene and prostitutes was so strong that in the late Middle Ages homes for prostitutes looking for a new life were called magdalenes.[11]

The truth is that there is no evidence that Mary Magdalene was ever a prostitute or that she was the sinner woman of Luke. What we do know is that Mary was a devout follower of Jesus Christ, the most faithful among his disciples, and possibly even his bride. But she was so much more than that.

Apocryphal texts recorded a very different Mary Magdalene. She was portrayed as fearless, questioning Jesus constantly, her appetite for knowledge insatiable. When the male disciples question her authenticity, she did not bend to their anger but stood firmly in her own power.

While the Virgin reflected the motherly aspect of the goddess, Mary Magdalene reintroduced Christianity to the fire of the Divine Feminine. And that fire swept through the ancient world where cults to Mary Magdalene flourished from Palestine to England. No human could ever hope to achieve the perfection of the Virgin Mary. She had been born unique to serve a unique purpose. But Mary Magdalene was fully human. And although nothing tangible connected her to the penitent prostitute, the image that association created drew people to her. Mary Magdalene was as broken and imperfect as everyone else. She sinned and repented. She tried and she failed. She wept, laughed, rejoiced, and mourned. She was not divine, but the divine had touched her in a way no other had experienced.

A goddess is rising. A new generation is searching for her within the Bible and finding not the Virgin, but Mary Magdalene. In her, women see a reflection of themselves. She is powerful yet soft. Vulnerable yet strong. She is intelligent, independent, and an equal to the men she moves among. Her story, though two thousand years old, continues to evolve. With the discovery of apocryphal texts like the Gospel of Mary, more are looking to her for wisdom and intercession. And like the goddesses of old, she welcomes all.

We are witnessing the birth of a goddess for the first time in millennia. Her story cannot be contained within a single chapter. No final words can summarize her reign as it has only just begun. The goddess is evolving, the fire of the Divine Feminine awaking. And her name is Mary Magdalene.

Chapter Seven

Goddess Found

From the dawn of humanity, people have sought the face of the divine. And quite often, it was the face of the goddess that was found, gently smiling back. She has been discovered in the darkest of caves, on the tallest of hills, and within great temples of gold and ivory. And although her voice has been weakened by centuries of neglect, her words still whisper to us in the raging of an angry sea and the quiet whisper of wind through her sacred trees.

Throughout human history savior gods have lived and died countless times. But those gods had always retained a connection to the goddess. Not to a subjugated goddess, but to one that stood as an equal in power and stature. Our ancestors saw the balance of nature reflected in the equality of the divine. And even the mightiest of warriors called upon the goddess in his hour of need without fear of ridicule or persecution.

For untold generations, the gods and goddesses of the world lived and evolved alongside humans. They fought the same battles, experienced the same joy and sorrow, and sought the same answers. Though their power was immeasurable, there was a spark of humanity in their souls that was easily recognizable. But nothing, it seems, lasts forever.

When the first small band of Hebrews raised their eyes and thoughts to Yahweh, humankind found themselves on a path that would redefine the entire cosmos. Although Yahweh himself never denied the existence of other gods and goddesses, he did demand unwavering loyalty among his chosen people. Often, by any means necessary. There was no weak humanity in the Hebrew God. He was beyond all knowing, indescribable, unattainable, and terrifying.

From the beginning, Yahweh set his sights on proving his

superiority among the more ancient deities. He easily assimilated the great god, El. He humiliated the storm god, Baal and took his spirit and epithets as his own. The goddess, however, proved a much tougher adversary. She would not be so easily cast aside for she filled the hearts of her people in a way that Yahweh never could. And they clung to her desperately.

For a while, it almost seemed that Yahweh was willing to make an exception for the beautiful Canaanite Asherah. She had been a worthy partner for El, and her presence at the side of Yahweh was welcomed among the people. Standing next to his altar, she reigned as the Queen of Heaven and the Bride of God for centuries. But Yahweh was a jealous god and inspired radical zealots that could not tolerate the presence of Asherah next to their Almighty God. They tore down her altars and crushed her standing stones. Her images were destroyed, her sacred places filled with the bones of her slaughtered faithful, and her worship outlawed.

Still, it was not enough. The early church fathers had discovered something dangerous in the goddess. The unwavering devotion she inspired in her followers threatened to rival the power of the omnipotent Yahweh. It would not be enough to eliminate Asherah herself for her spirit was reflected in the eyes and minds of all womankind.

The Israelites couldn't destroy the goddess, but they could certainly bury her essence. They stripped her down into the most basic aspects of her sex and thrust her into the Garden. Her creative powers were usurped by the Father God, her womb left desolate. She became the fall of humankind, the reason for all suffering and death in a world of chaos. She became the evil, inherent she-demon hiding within every female heart. Just as the faithful man had been warned against the wiles of the blasphemous goddess, he came to fear and despise the weakness she had bestowed upon all women. The subjugation of womankind reflected the abatement of the goddess. Every woman bore the curse of the first.

But altars are easily rebuilt, and the hearts of the people are not so easily swayed. The goddess endured, even when seemingly forgotten. She found subtle and clever ways to enter the domain of the Hebrew God and evolved to fit within the new reality of the world. She became the dwelling of God, his physical presence in the world he created but could not inhabit. Yahweh could not walk among his people, but the goddess could. And they gathered eagerly within her outstretched arms, starved of the Divine Feminine for so long.

The goddesses covered within this book are not alone in the story of the Hebrews. The Phoenician Astarte, the Semitic Anath, and the Egyptian Isis all contributed to the development of Judaism as did countless others. Their stories and powers merged with and enhanced Asherah just as they had each evolved from even more ancient goddesses. Within the holy writings of the Bible, along with midrashic and apocryphal literature, even more goddess-like figures emerged. Like the Shekinah and Mary, these were true Hebrew demigoddesses – Israel (the personified community), the Word, the Sabbath, the Daughter of Zion, and even the Torah itself emerged as unique characters within the Judeo-Christian faith. And each of them were distinctly female.[1]

Over the last several decades, scholars and theologians have wrestled with the idea of an Israelite goddess. The entirety of the Jewish and Christian faiths rely, after all, on Yahweh as the one and only deity. And although many of the faithful still do not acknowledge or even know of the possibility of her existence, the historical evidence provides a definitive answer. There *was* a Hebrew goddess who stood as the equal of Yahweh.[2] She was his wife, his lover, the source of His creation, and the mother of the faithful. The Promised Land was filled with her altars upon every high hill and beneath every green tree. Great kings bowed before her while women throughout Israel and Judah baked cakes in her honor. Her image can still be seen in ancient votive offerings found throughout the Holy Land. She brought love, vitality, protection, and fertility to her people.

Beginning in the 1970s, a movement began to spread throughout North America, Europe, and Australia. Known simply as the Goddess Movement, women around the world began to question their assigned roles within primarily male-dominated religions. A shift began to take place toward female-led religious experiences, and the goddess was reintroduced to a new generation of eager women searching for the feminine face of God.

St. Paul, in the first letter of Timothy, had written that women must be quiet and submissive. But women had been quieted for centuries, and some are finding it difficult to remain that way any longer. Feminist movements have swept through religious and secular arenas throughout the world, opening long overdue dialog about the equality of man and woman. Within some branches of the church, women are being placed in positions of leadership never before afforded to them. Some Jewish sects have worked to eliminate gender-specific terminology from their definition of Yahweh, asserting that Yahweh is (and always has been) beyond gender labels. The progress has been positive but much work is left to do.

Many in the Goddess Movement would come to identify themselves as neopagans, Wiccans, or pantheists, separating themselves from the traditional patriarchal religions. But incredibly, the idea of a female godhead began to take root in the Jewish and Christian communities as well. Women are studying their faiths in greater detail than ever, and finding their outdated pretenses about their sex abhorrent. Delving deeper into the history of their faiths, women are again and again finding themselves in the presence of a forgotten goddess.

For many, just as it was for me, discovering the Israelite goddess is a profound experience. For once she has been recognized, it becomes easier to spot her shadowed movements throughout the Bible and other religious texts. Her spirit is reflected in the strong women of the Old Testament – Esther, Deborah, Miriam, and others. Her symbols and holy places permeate the landscape and hints of her worship hide within words unspoken. Her own innate glory resonates throughout time, drawing to her those that are simply seeking something *more.*

But why does the goddess matter at all? Why now, after millennia of silence, is her voice important? For feminists, the answer is obvious. She matters because she stood as an equal to a powerful God. She was not born to serve. She was not property to buy or sale. She inhabited her own power and worked according to her own will – things that even modern women still struggle with. But it is not just to those seeking equality that she calls. Men, as well, have heard the gentle call of the Mother Goddess and are finding solace in her loving embrace. For generations, boys have been told that to become a "man" they must leave their mothers and childhoods behind, toughening themselves for the harsh world that awaits them. In the Middle Ages, this became the Hero's Quest, a search for the Father beyond the grasp of the Mother. It is an idea that has permeated western civilization and shaped the path of countless men. And that separation from the Mother has left them incomplete, just as it has for so many women. Women seek the goddess for self-empowerment. Men seek her for the love and acceptance that can only be found in the heart of a mother.

For at least the last two thousand years, life has been reflected through the prism of the Yahwistic faiths. Civilizations have been built on the tenets found in the Holy Bible. Entire cultures have been ravaged and decimated in the name of God. People have been enslaved, women have been stoned, children have been stolen. Yahweh is a ruthless god, only somewhat tempered by his son, Jesus, and his teachings of love and acceptance. Perhaps, now more than ever, the reemergence of the goddess is desperately needed. Tracing her journey through the Biblical events that have molded the world around us illustrates that what we have been taught is only part of the story. There is still much to learn and discover.

For some, no amount of evidence will ever be enough to convince them that Asherah and so many other goddesses ever walked beside Yahweh. This entire book will seem blasphemous and full of wickedness designed to lead the faithful astray. But that was never the intention. Instead, this book is meant as a starting point for those whose hearts are open enough to ask "what if?"

Asherah may have begun as a wholly Canaanite deity, but by the end of her journey she had become undeniably Christian. Born again as the Holy Mother, the goddess reclaimed her ancient status as the Queen of Heaven. Just as Asherah had reigned next to her son, Baal, Mary emerged as co-redeemer with her son, Jesus. Together, they ushered in a new human era that continues to shape the foundations of the world.

But then again, perhaps this is not the end of her story. The goddess is very much alive, and her presence is growing. In recent years, interest in the Virgin has begun to shift to another Mary. As the Magdalene story grows, as belief in her as the bride of Jesus and the most beloved among his disciples evolves, perhaps she will emerge as the next incarnation of the goddess. Only one thing is for certain – the goddess is hidden no longer.

Notes

General Notes:

Throughout the text, Yahweh/God/The Lord are used interchangeably.

All Biblical quotes are from the New International Version.

Chapter One: The Quest Begins

1. Armstrong 1993
2. Exodus 19:18
3. Exodus 20:3
4. Armstrong 1993
5. Patai 1990
6. Armstrong 1993
7. Patai 1990
8. Patai 1990

Chapter Two: The Queen

1. Dever 2005
2. Patai 1990
3. Patai 1990
4. Judges 6:30
5. Patai 1990
6. 1 Kings 2:2-3
7. 1 Kings 3:3
8. Dever 2005
9. 1 Kings 8:23
10. 1 Kings 11:2
11. 1 Kings 11:4
12. 1 Kings 11:37
13. 1 Kings 14:22-23
14. 2 Chronicles 14:3-5
15. 1 Kings 15:13

16. 1 Kings 15:14; 2 Chronicles 15:17
17. 2 Chronicles 14:2
18. 1 Kings 11:37
19. 1 Kings 12:28
20. 1 Kings 16:32-33
21. 1 Kings 18:19
22. 1 Kings 18:22-24
23. 2 Kings 12:2
24. 2 Kings 12:3
25. 2 Chronicles 24:18
26. 2 Kings 13:2
27. 2 Kings 13:6
28. Patai 1990
29. 2 Kings 18:4
30. 2 Chronicles 29:5
31. 2 Kings 18:5
32. 2 Kings 18:7
33. 2 Chronicles 33:3
34. 2 Kings 21:7
35. Deuteronomy 12:2-3
36. 2 Kings 23:4
37. 2 Kings 23:6, 2 Chronicles 34:4
38. 2 Kings 23:7
39. 2 Kings 23:14

Chapter Three: The Genesis

1. Genesis 1:1
2. Genesis 1:27
3. Genesis 2:5
4. Genesis 2:7
5. Genesis 2:9
6. Genesis 2:16-17
7. Genesis 2:19
8. Genesis 2:21-22

9. Genesis 2:23
10. Patai 1990
11. Patai 1990
12. Patai 1990
13. Koltuv 1986
14. Patai 1990, Koltuv 1986
15. Genesis 3:1
16. Genesis 3:2-3
17. Genesis 3:5
18. Genesis 3:6
19. Genesis 3:7
20. Genesis 3:11
21. Genesis 3:12
22. Genesis 3:13
23. Genesis 3:16
24. Genesis 3:20
25. Genesis 3:24
26. Genesis 3:19
27. Ezekiel 18:20
28. Armstrong 1993
29. 1 Timothy 2:11-14
30. Pughe 2007
31. Shabbath 151b
32. Patai 1990
33. Unterman 1991
34. Patai 1990

Chapter Four – The Glory

1. Unterman 1991
2. Armstrong 1993
3. Patai 1990
4. Proverbs 8:24-26
5. Matthews 2001
6. Matthews 2001

7. Proverbs 1:26
8. Proverbs 1:31
9. Matthews 2001
10. Patai 1990
11. Patai 1990
12. Armstrong 1993
13. Exodus 25:22
14. Patai 1990
15. 1 Kings 6:13
16. Este 2010
17. 1 Kings 8:10
18. Patai 1990
19. Patai 1990
20. Patai 1990
21. Armstrong 1993
22. Patai 1990
23. Patai 1990
24. Patai 1990
25. Patai 1990
26. Patai 1990
27. Patai 1990
28. Luke 2:9
29. 2 Corinthians 2:8
30. Patai 1990

Chapter Five – The Mother

1. Luke 1:28
2. Luke 1:30-32
3. Luke 1:34
4. Luke 1:38
5. Luke 1:43
6. Matthew 1:20
7. Matthew 1:25
8. Luke 2:11-12

9. Luke 2:19
10. Luke 2:29-32
11. Luke 2:34-35
12. Luke 2:48
13. Luke 2:49
14. John 2:4
15. Luke 8:21
16. Ashe 1976
17. Warner 1983
18. Warner 1983
19. Matthew 1:25
20. Warner 1983, Ashe 1976
21. Warner 1983
22. Warner 1983, Ashe 1976
23. Warner 1983
24. Ashe 1976
25. Ashe 1976
26. Warner 1983
27. Warner 1983
28. Ashe 1976
29. Warner 1983, Ashe 1976

Chapter Six – The Heiress

1. Luke 8:1-3
2. Luke 8:3
3. Haag 2016
4. John 20:1-10
5. John 20:13
6. John 20:15
7. John 20:16
8. Matthew 28:1-10, Mark 16:1-8, Luke 24:1-8
9. Haag 2016
10. Luke 7:47
11. Warner 1983

Chapter Six – Goddess Found

1. Patai 1990
2. Dever 2005

Select Bibliography

Armstrong, Karen. (1993). *A History of God*. New York, NY: Ballantine Books.

Ashe, Geoffrey. (1976). *The Virgin*. Stroud, Gloucestershire: The History Press Ltd.

Dever, William G. (2005). *Did God Have a Wife?* Grand Rapids, MI: William B. Eerdmans Publishing Co.

Dever, William, G. (2003). *Who Were the Early Israelites and Where Did They Come From?* Grand Rapids, MI: William B. Eerdmans Publishing Co.

Este, Sorita & Rankine, David. (2010). *The Cosmic Shekinah*. London, England: Avalonia.

Frymer-Kensky, Tikva. (1992). *In the Wake of the Goddesses*. New York, NY: Ballantine Books.

Gadon, Elinor W. (1989) *The Once and Future Goddess*. San Francisco, CA: HarperSanFrancisco.

Haag, Michael. (2016). *The Quest for Mary Magdalene*. New York, NY: HarperCollins Publishing.

Hurwitz, Siegmund. (2012). *Lilith-The First Eve*. Zurich, Switzerland: Daimon Verlag.

Husain, Shahrukh. (1997). *The Goddess*. London, England: Duncan Baird Publishers.

Kirsch, Jonathan. (2004). *God Against the Gods*. New York, NY: Penguin Group.

Koltuv, Barbara Black. (1986). *The Book of Lilith*. York Beach, ME: Nicholas-Hays Inc.

Matthews, Caitlin. (2001). *Sophia*. Wheaton, IL: Quest Books.

Patai, Raphael. (1990). *The Hebrew Goddess*. Detroit, MI: University Press.

Pughe, Roberta Mary & Sohl, Paula Anema. (2007). *Resurrecting Eve*. Ashland, OR: White Cloud Press.

Raver, Miki. (1998). *Listen to Her Voice*. San Francisco, CA:

Chronicle Books.

Smith, Mark S. (2002) *The Early History of God.* Grand Rapids, MI: William B Eerdmans Publishing Co.

Unterman, Alan. (1991). *Dictionary of Jewish Lore and Legend.* New York, NY: Thames and Hudson, Ltd.

Warner, Marina. (1983). *Alone of All Her Sex.* New York: Random House.

**MOON
BOOKS**

PAGANISM & SHAMANISM

What is Paganism? A religion, a spirituality, an alternative
belief system, nature worship? You can find support for all these
definitions (and many more) in dictionaries, encyclopaedias, and
text books of religion, but subscribe to any one and the truth will
evade you. Above all Paganism is a creative pursuit, an encounter
with reality, an exploration of meaning and an expression of the
soul. Druids, Heathens, Wiccans and others, all contribute their
insights and literary riches to the Pagan tradition. Moon Books
invites you to begin or to deepen your own encounter, right here,
right now.
If you have enjoyed this book, why not tell other readers by
posting a review on your preferred book site.

Medicine for the Soul
The Complete Book of Shamanic Healing
Ross Heaven
All you will ever need to know about shamanic healing and how to
become your own shaman...
Paperback: 978-1-78099-419-2 ebook: 978-1-78099-420-8

Shaman Pathways – The Druid Shaman
Exploring the Celtic Otherworld
Danu Forest
A practical guide to Celtic shamanism with exercises and
techniques as well as traditional lore for exploring the Celtic
Otherworld.
Paperback: 978-1-78099-615-8 ebook: 978-1-78099-616-5

Traditional Witchcraft for the Woods and Forests
A Witch's Guide to the Woodland with Guided Meditations and
Pathworking
Mélusine Draco
A Witch's guide to walking alone in the woods, with guided
meditations and pathworking.
Paperback: 978-1-84694-803-9 ebook: 978-1-84694-804-6

Wild Earth, Wild Soul
A Manual for an Ecstatic Culture
Bill Pfeiffer
Imagine a nature-based culture so alive and so connected,
spreading like wildfire. This book is the first flame...
Paperback: 978-1-78099-187-0 ebook: 978-1-78099-188-7

Naming the Goddess
Trevor Greenfield
Naming the Goddess is written by over eighty adherents and
scholars of Goddess and Goddess Spirituality.
Paperback: 978-1-78279-476-9 ebook: 978-1-78279-475-2

Shapeshifting into Higher Consciousness
Heal and Transform Yourself and Our World with Ancient
Shamanic and Modern Methods
Llyn Roberts
Ancient and modern methods that you can use every day to
transform yourself and make a positive difference in the world.
Paperback: 978-1-84694-843-5 ebook: 978-1-84694-844-2

Readers of ebooks can buy or view any of these bestsellers by
clicking on the live link in the title. Most titles are published in
paperback and as an ebook. Paperbacks are available in traditional
bookshops. Both print and ebook formats are available online.

Find more titles and sign up to our readers' newsletter at
http://www.johnhuntpublishing.com/paganism
Follow us on Facebook at https://www.facebook.com/MoonBooks
and Twitter at https://twitter.com/MoonBooksJHP